One Great Society

Books by Howard Mumford Jones

Reflections on Learning

American Humanism

The Theory of American Literature

A Guide to American Literature and Its Backgrounds since 1890

The Pursuit of Happiness

The Bright Medusa

Education and World Tragedy

Ideas in America

America and French Culture, 1750–1848

The Frontier in American Fiction

with others   Modern Minds

editor   A Primer of Intellectual Freedom

with others, editor   Major American Writers

HOWARD MUMFORD JONES # One

Great Society

HUMANE LEARNING IN THE UNITED STATES

HARCOURT, BRACE & COMPANY · NEW YORK

PREFACE

This book is not about teaching except incidentally and indirectly, but it concerns something fundamental to both teaching and civilization; namely, how do you maintain and enrich the organized knowledge about the achievements of mankind over the centuries, upon which teaching depends? It is, to make a bad play on words, not about teaching but about learning. It concerns those vast areas of human knowledge that lie outside the physical, natural, and mathematical sciences, the fields we vaguely call the humanities. (The relations, or some of the relations, of the social sciences to the humanities will also form part of the story.) There is presently a great deal of excitement in the air about the education of scientists; this book concerns the education of their counterparts, the scholars. Language perpetually betrays us, and it does here. The distinction between scientist and scholar is approximate, not absolute. Many scholars use scientific instruments and modes of analysis for the solution of professional problems, and many scientists bring scholarly knowledge to bear upon scientific work. But the distinction, though empirical only, is sufficient for our purposes. This book is not about the teacher, but about the scholar. This fact does not mean that teaching is neglected.

By the same token, this book is about humanistic scholarship and not about contemporary art and artists and "creativity." To a European scholar this disclaimer would be

v

bewildering. In Europe art is one thing, and scholarship another thing. But in the United States our colleges and universities are coming more and more to be patrons of the arts. One may take various views of this development, and the situation is far more complicated than most persons realize. The important thing, however, is not to confuse the purposes of scholarship with the support of living artists in university chairs. Scholarship exists in its own right. It is fundamental to art or, if one prefers, to the arts. Scholarship should, and does, concern itself about recent and contemporary art. But that is not the only thing scholarship is about. Scholarship conserves the past of the arts and of civilization.

This book, then, is about humane learning. Other matters are necessarily incidental.

. . .

It is a commonplace that in the United States the support of scientific research and of research in the social sciences far outweighs the support given scholarly research in the humanities. The nineteenth-century American scholar—James Russell Lowell, William Dwight Whitney, and Charles Eliot Norton are examples—enjoyed a prestige that in the twentieth century has passed to the physicist and the social scientist. Ours is a scientific age, a technological age, ours is an age conscious of "social adjustment," international tensions, and the pressures of social forces upon the individual. It is also an age haunted by the fear of the total destruction of mankind. It would seem essential in such an age, therefore, to review the cultural tradition that ought to bring us wisdom, beauty, tolerance, and virtue, and the theory of humane learning on which the tradition depends. Such is the purpose of this statement about learning, authorized by a Commission on the Humanities of the American Council of Learned Societies.

The Commission, operating under the chairmanship of the writer, was composed of Americans chosen because they could bring to bear upon the problem of the relation of humane learning to the national culture a variety of points of view. The membership was as follows:

Whitney J. Oates,
  Vice-Chairman
Harvie Branscomb
Lawrence H. Chamberlain
William C. De Vane
Charles W. Hendel
Pendleton Herring

Arthur A. Houghton, Jr.
Robert Oppenheimer
Louis M. Rabinowitz
Roger H. Sessions
Francis Henry Taylor
Robert Ulich

It is melancholy to have to record that Mr. Rabinowitz and Mr. Taylor died before this report appeared. Each contributed importantly to the deliberations of the Commission.

Professor Oates brought to bear upon our discussions the point of view of a classicist. Dr. Branscomb in some measure represented the relations between the humanities and religion. Dean Chamberlain was appointed as particularly representing political science. Dean De Vane is of course a student of literature, and Professor Hendel is a teacher of philosophy. Dr. Herring represents the friendly interest of the social sciences. Mr. Houghton represents the concern of an enlightened business mind about education. Mr. Oppenheimer, needless to remark, is a philosophical scientist. Mr. Rabinowitz, like Mr. Houghton, represented the interests of business, and was also a bibliophile. Mr. Sessions was named to the Commission to represent the living arts, and Mr. Taylor to represent the standpoint of the historian and scholar of the fine arts. Mr. Ulich is an exponent of the philosophy of education. These distinguished men were drawn together by a concern for the greatness of learning. Their deliberations were made possible by two generous grants from the Carnegie Corporation.

The Commission met monthly during most of 1955 and 1956 (except for the summers), and in the spring of 1956 held a three-day session at the Worcester Museum of Art, Worcester, Massachusetts, made possible by the profound concern of Francis Henry Taylor for the success of the Commission. This was attended by the Commission, by the board of directors of the American Council of Learned Societies and members of the staff of that organization, and by other scholars and administrators invited from all parts of the United States. The record of this meeting, the records of the meetings of the Commission proper and of its committees, notes on conversations with other scholars, scientists, social scientists, and men of affairs, and reading in the vast, vague library of "literature" about education and about the humanities are the basis of this book. From August, 1957 through January, 1958, the writer was a Fellow of the Center for Advanced Study of the Behavioral Sciences at Stanford, California. As preliminary drafts of chapters were written, these were circulated among the nearly fifty Fellows at the Center, subjected to their criticism, and reworked in the light of suggestions thus received. I owe a debt of gratitude to the Fellows and to the Director of the Center, Dr. Ralph W. Tyler. Thanks are also due to the staff members of the American Council of Learned Societies; and to Mr. John F. Freeman of Harvard University and to Miss Miriam Gallaher of the Center for patient and intelligent research, much of it over and beyond the call of duty. Thanks are likewise due to Professor Richard M. Ludwig of Princeton University for his critical reading of many chapters.

It is impossible to name the many scholars who have read part or all of this report in manuscript, but I owe special thanks to Professor Henry Nash Smith, Professor Mark Schorer, and Professor Adrienne Koch of the University of California at Berkeley; and to Professor John W. Dodds and Professor Thomas Moser of Stanford University for searching comment on particular passages.

This statement is authorized by the Commission. That is to say, the Commission, desirous of a unified report, instructed its Chairman to speak for the whole body, though not necessarily to reflect every difference of opinion among the members of the Commission. This he has tried to do. Not all members of the Commission necessarily agree with everything that is said here, but the general drift of the argument is, he believes, what the Commission intends to put before the public. The style, form, and substance of the report are the Chairman's individual responsibility.

A philologist cannot hope to compete with an atomic physicist for acclaim or for support, nor does this report make any such assumption. It does assume, however, that there is a limit of neglect below which a great nation cannot afford to sink its support of humane learning. This book is intended to help restore balance, not in the sense of taking his money away from the scientist or his key position in government or business from the social scientist, but in the sense of indicating that, wonderful as science is and influential as are the social sciences, they are not the whole of culture. Thoughtful scientists and social scientists never argue that they are. But that portion of the public which is essentially concerned about the drift of American values is not perhaps as fully informed about the theory and practice of humane learning as it would like to be; and it is to such citizens that this volume is directed.

HOWARD MUMFORD JONES

Harvard University
April 28, 1958

There is
One great society alone on earth;
The noble Living and the noble Dead.
—*The Prelude,* XI:393–95

CONTENTS

1. Concerning the Humanities

ONE

What Are the Humanities?

Most of us are aware that knowledge is divided into three large categories—the sciences (including mathematics), the social sciences, and the humanities.[1] Most of us have a fair working knowledge of science, or if not that, of what science is about, and many of us have a practical acquaintance with some of the social sciences—for example, economics. The same kind of acquaintance is not so general where the humanities are concerned. A leading businessman, sympathetic with the purpose of humane learning, asked what questions business leaders would presumably want answered if they were called upon to support scholarship in this field, began, in fact, by making this his leading question:

[1] This division leaves out theology. The simplest definition of theology is the knowledge of God, but another definition is "the critical, historical, and psychological study of religion and religious ideas." In many American colleges this approach to religious ideas is, as it were, distributed among philosophy, history, literature, and other departments, a distribution in part forced upon tax-supported institutions by constitutional provisions separating church and state. Privately endowed colleges and universities, even though they may include a school of theology, often follow suit so far as the general instruction of undergraduates is concerned. Theology as part of the professional preparation of a minister or priest for his sacred calling is confined to divinity schools in the main. The situation in the Roman Catholic colleges, however, retains the medieval doctrine of the supremacy of theology. But see pp. 12–15 and 167–170 below.

1. What are the humanities?

2. Are the humanities something different from the subjects of English, history, languages, and the like that we took at school and college?

3. Why is it that you think the humanities are so important?

4. Haven't the humanities always existed? Why should there be such an attempt at emphasis on them at the present time?

5. Speaking quite practically, what can the humanities do for me, for my family, for my business, for my community?

6. If I were interested, how could I learn more about the humanities? Do the facilities exist in my typical community? If not, where do I turn?

7. Do the humanities make people better? Do they make people happier? Do they make people more capable? How do you know?

8. What could be done in our community to increase knowledge of the humanities? Specifically, what should be done in our local schools? In our public library? In the program of local clubs and institutions?

9. What would be the best way for the business world to assist the humanities? Are there specific projects that should be supported, similar to scientific projects? Or are scholarships the answer?

10. Can the humanities be applied in some fashion to our business? To our community life?

11. I feel I have a responsibility as a business leader and a citizen to apply time and energy, and support the things that are worth while. Are you suggesting things that will take my time, energy, support? If so, why should they have priority over my present interests that help keep the community running?

These are intelligent questions. Asked by a businessman for businessmen, they could as easily have come from a labor leader, a social worker, an engineer, a politician, a clergyman, a scientist, or a housewife. It does not affect the excellence of the questions that some of them are unanswerable. In the matter of happiness, as Thackeray long ago observed, which of us has his desires, or having them, is satisfied? Others of them which look easy—for example, what can be done in our local schools, or our public library, or in local clubs and institutions?—are rather difficult questions because answers must go back to what one feels the general philosophy of culture, the general values of American life, truly are. Obviously, there is no use setting up a particular program unless and until you know why you are setting it up. Let us, however, begin trying to answer some of these questions.

The prevailing anxiety in the United States today is fear lest some trigger-happy member of our own armed forces (or of the Russian) may in a moment of anger or bewilderment make a mistake, drop a bomb, and set off World War III. In that event, it is calmly said, few of us will live to tell the tale. Millions on millions of Americans will die in agony—but so will millions on millions of human beings who are not Americans. Our cities will be reduced to obscene rubble, our water supply will be contaminated, most of the land will be for an indefinite period filled with deadly or crippling radiation, the fish in the sea will be inedible, and it is even said that in that mad moment we may see—or, rather, we shall not be there to see—the end of human life on this planet.

This is not the imagining of a lurid writer of scientific fantasies. It is a cold, sober possibility. Speaking in Washington in November, 1957, General Omar N. Bradley, who is not an excitable person, had this to say:

The central problem of our time—as I view it—is how to employ human intelligence for the salvation of mankind. It is a problem we have put upon ourselves. For we have defiled our intellect by the creation of such scientific instruments of destruction that we are now in desperate danger of destroying ourselves. Our plight is critical and with each effort we have made to relieve it by further scientific advances, we have succeeded only in aggravating our peril. As a result, we are now speeding inexorably toward a day when even the ingenuity of our scientists may be unable to save us from the consequences of a single rash act or a lone reckless hand upon the switch of an uninterceptible missile.

Unless we change our ways, he warned, all we can hope to do is to "smother our fears and attempt to live in a thickening shadow of death." He pleaded for encouraging another kind of intelligence in order to solve the central problem of our time: how to preserve the planet on which we live. But if the ingenuity of our scientists seems less able to save us than once it did, it seems clear that we may be following some wrongheaded philosophy about the nature of life and of civilization. We need to try something else, some other philosophy. The study of philosophy is one of the central studies of the humanities.

If we look away from the military problem, we find ourselves confronting a social world of infinite complexity. The universe of business, industry, and finance, for reasons so intricate that neither economists nor social psychologists have ever quite mastered them, seems to undergo mysterious movements of expansion and contraction, boom and bust, prosperity and depression. We struggle with these phenomena. We try to regulate them through the discount rate or the interest rate or through government spending, and we hope we know a little more about the matter each time a depression occurs, but we also have to face the fact that so many workers are bound to be unemployed, so many firms will fail, so many persons will go through bankruptcy. We have problems of juvenile delinquency in our vast city schools, and social workers can, and do, furnish us tables measuring the increase or decrease of juvenile delinquency in the country as a whole or by states or by cities. We have, or can make, curves that show the rate of highway fatalities caused by traffic accidents, the numbers of marriages and divorces in the United States, the rate of increase in population in the world, the country, the state, the county, the city. We can find out all sorts of things by the statistical methods used in social studies and in science, and we can even predict (by the process known as extrapolation) with a high degree of probability how many persons are going to want to enter college, how many persons will buy motorcycles, how many smokers will buy cigarettes, how many patients will need hospital care, and how many Americans will, in the normal course of things, die in such and such a period of time. Our capacity to make such studies and to predict probable events of this sort is great and will in all probability increase if we survive at all. History is a one-way process, so that we cannot know whether the business recessions of the past would have been shorter or easier to bear if statesmen, economists, social workers, legislators, administrators, and others had had the kind of predictive statistical analysis possible to us today. Always, of course, if we survive.

But though we can say with considerable confidence that so many persons will be killed or crippled on our highways in such and such a year, we cannot predict of a particular person that he will be killed. We can expect such and such an amount of vandalism in the slums of this or that city, but we cannot surely say that John Johnson, Jesús Maria Buenosangre, Stefan Prodopoulos, or Winnie Mae O'Toole is going to be "bad." We cannot even know what dark drives in the soul of this or that juvenile delinquent required the satisfaction of crime; we cannot know the passionate hungers, the loneliness, the frustration that send one lad to the reform school and another up the river. We can find out that so many small businesses are sure to fail in the United States in the next six months, but we cannot experience the shame of failure, the stigma, the wretchedness, the bewilderment of this or that small merchant who, putting all his moral force into the enterprise and playing the game according to the rules as he understood them, was nevertheless beaten by the blind fates and was tempted like Job to curse God and die. The figures on marriage and divorce, the birth rate, abortions, and so on, are highly technical and useful instruments of analysis; they do not throw a single ray of light upon the profound human emotions that lay behind each marriage, each birth, each divorce, each abortion. Brilliant social analysis helps us in some measure to guide the development of society, but it commonly fails to tell us why we are our brother's keeper —if, indeed, we are—just as it fails to illuminate the full meaning of Wesley's famous and terrible phrase "There but for the grace of God go I."

Men die daily, even without the help of hydrogen bombs to usher them out of the world by millions, but they do not really die by millions, they die alone. Men live in crowds, societies, and states, and we can compute a good many facts about them, but they do not really live in multitudes; they live apart, each in the secret chamber of himself. The figures on the birth rate indicate that we shall have to build more schools; they do not indicate that each of these individual babies comes into the world alone. The experience of being a child is a private experience, and so is the experience of marriage, the experience of bearing a child, the experience of boredom, the experience of rapture, the experience of loss. Personalities are not made by statistics but are something unique and apart. The great moments of life are commonly solitary moments. Then it is that we call upon the experience of beauty or of faith to get us through, then it is that the support of philosophy or ethics or art really counts. When all the loud noises of the world of sports and business and politics fall away, the thoughtful soul retires to a solitude that neither chemistry nor economics can invade. Man in these moments of insight sees himself simultaneously as a lonely voyager upon the sea of existence and as a part of the human race. He is then not so much a member of the stock exchange, the vice-chairman of the governing board of Utopia College, a foreman in an airplane factory, or a cattle-raiser in Wyoming; he sees himself in these moments of insight in a perspective of time, as one in the procession of men on this planet, whether in the United States or on the most distant islands of the sea.

2

The primary business of the humanities is to make the human heritage man looks back upon meaningful and available as individual experience rather than as mass and generalization. The purpose of humane learning is to offer those wise enough to want to accept the lesson of human experience an interpretation of the life of man—its tragedies and aspirations, its brutalities and its comic relief. The lesson of human experience in this sense constitutes whatever wisdom man has learned from the processes of history and from those enduring expressions or interpretations of experience we call philosophy, religion in a broad and generous sense, works of literature, and works in the fine arts, including music, architecture, and the dance.

The scientist studies the structure of the human body (and of course an infinite number of things besides). He also studies the human psyche so far as this can be known to him through question and answer, stimulus and response, introspection and record. The social scientist necessarily views man principally as a social being, reporting upon his behavior in terms of group and custom, pattern, belief, and tradition. But there is forever something elusive that escapes both modes of interpretation. It is true that each of us knows he can be made the subject of scientific analysis, as when he consults a doctor or a psychiatrist, just as each of us knows only too well he is a member of society—a voter, a laborer, an employer, a churchgoer, a member of a club, and so on and so on. But each of us also knows, deep down and underneath, that he is something or somebody neither the doctor nor the sociologist can quite get at. He knows himself *as* a self, a self shaped in important ways by nature and by society, but a self that is more than the product of physiology and social conditioning. This self has its independent and interior life, its taciturn and private views and values. To itself, at any rate, this self seems to stand outside natural processes and to be more than the sum of its behavior. Against all argument designed to prove that this transcendent being is not transcendent and that man is not and cannot be a free spirit, the self incorrigibly and illogically (if necessary) insists that it *is*.

We know this well enough. On one plane this general truth occasions things like James Thurber's amusing narrative about the strange, secret life of Walter Mitty. On another plane the self knows itself as a mind creating knowledge, directing activity, earning a living, and so on. On still another plane the self is a spirit capable of withdrawing from the whole thing, as in Buddhism, or as desirous to be saved, as in Christianity, or as something to be ethically disciplined by family and state traditions as in Confucianism, or as an original, innate participant in "human nature," as in Greek thought. "Human nature" can never be satisfactorily defined. Extreme arguments are set forth about it. It is argued by one school that our sense of difference from all the rest of nature is sheer illusion, and by another school that man may, indeed, be *in* nature but that he is not wholly *of* nature. That part of him which is not *of* nature is spiritual; and the doctrine of the double nature of man has played an important part in the development of human cultures. Much of the material of the humanities springs from the theory of the dualism of man, who is according to this doctrine mind and body, spirit and body, soul and body, the antithesis varying according to the cultural or religious or philosophical tradition of one or another race or nation.[2]

3

What are the humanities? They include philosophy in all its branches (such as ethics, logic, and epistemology—the theory of knowledge), the languages, literature in all its varied aspects, music, the fine arts, the decorative arts, the arts of the theater. Certain aspects of anthropology and folklore are of interest to humane learning. So are many of the philosophical aspects of science and the social sciences, but we need not here enter upon this perplexing problem of definition further than to dwell for a minute

[2] The material studied by humanists includes, of course, not merely the expressions of philosophic dualism but also the expressions of philosophic monism. A "materialist" is not necessarily an ignoble fellow, nor is an "agnostic" necessarily without the highest ethical aims. Nor can the historic interest of humane learning in idealistic philosophy be construed to mean that science and the social sciences are "materialistic." The fact that the material studied by the humanist often has to do with man's faith in a supernatural order does not mean, on the other hand, that the humanist per se has an uncritical faith in this or that order of supernaturalism. Humane learning values any expression of a noble faith in life, whether or not that faith rests upon supernatural assumptions or upon more nearly temporal values, as was sometimes the case with the Greeks and the Romans.

upon the ambiguous position of history. So far as the writing of history is the product of art, it belongs with literature and therefore with the humanities. So far as the interpretation of history rests upon philosophical assumptions about man, human nature, and the purpose, principles, or patterns in history, history belongs with the humanities by partaking of the character of philosophy. So far as history employs statistical methodology or other analytical instruments forged by the social scientist, it belongs with social science.[3] But the humanities depend for their very existence upon perspective in time, so that history is the essence of their being. If the situation seems confusing, a moment's reflection will show how it came about. Let us take both an ancient and a modern example. In the case of Plato we have a great philosophical and literary figure whose works include *The Republic,* one of the foundation books in the development of political science as a social science. Contrariwise, in the case of John Stuart Mill we have one of the masters of nineteenth-century political economy and, simultaneously, one of the masters of Victorian prose. You cannot leave Plato and Mill and others like them out of the social sciences, but neither can you leave them out of the humanities.

Since theology is, briefly, knowledge of God, and since it has just been said that a body-soul philosophy underlies the creation of many works commonly studied in the humanities, it may well be asked why theology is not included in this part of learning. The answer has to be made in historical terms. From the fall of the Roman Empire of the West in the fifth century to the discovery of printing in the Western world in the fifteenth century, there was gradually built up by the Roman Catholic church and the medieval universities a unified system of thought known as

[3] In a general sense, it is clear, what is said of history is also true of many branches of learning more commonly classed as social science.

scholasticism, dominant in the West from the twelfth into the fifteenth centuries. Scholasticism fused into a single whole Christian theology and what was then believed to be true of the theories of Aristotle. Its methods were analytical rather than observational (though this is not literally true in every respect), the development of new modes of knowledge was sometimes crippled by authoritarianism, and by the middle of the fifteenth century it had ceased to be a fruitful method of acquiring new knowledge. Another attitude toward life, literature, and learning had begun to develop in the Mediterranean world even before 1450. Why should everything be referred to the priestly caste? Why should not men live their own lives as human beings rather than as souls possibly doomed to damnation? Why not look around you instead of first looking into the books of the scholastics to see if it was allowed to look around you? Ancient writings were discovered, rediscovered, or revalued, writings by the great spirits of Greece and Rome who could not possibly have been Christians but who nevertheless were among the noblest of mankind. These men had created art and literature, constructed systems of philosophy and science, built empires, and developed civilizations through the wise application of the powers of man to the persistent problems of humanity. They represented a lofty development of mankind.

Knowledge of these individuals and knowledge arising from the interpretation of their work got to be known as humanism, and was by this term distinguished from theology. Humanism sought not only to understand the past through the reinterpretation of the cultures of Greece and Rome, it sought also to apply these studies to the development of culture contemporary with the humanists, first by rather narrow imitations of the ancients, and afterward by infusing into the art and thought of the fifteenth and later centuries the lessons learned from these examples. Since the rediscovery, reinterpretation, and revaluation of the Greek and Latin world seemed to reveal an admirable phase of human life, humanism at first confined itself to the ways by which the ancient world could be interpreted, so that the original humanists were what today we would call professors of the classical languages. But the concept of humanism gradually broadened to mean not only the interpretation of any relevant part of the human story, but also ways by which, in the light of this interpretation, human nature could be enriched and matured. By the nineteenth century the "humanities" were no longer confined to classical studies, and in our century, though the culture of the ancient world is still important, the totality of man's past, the arts, languages, and philosophies of many cultures, philosophy in its most general scope, and the teaching and practice of the criticism and appreciation of the arts are the principal humanities. Moreover, the humanist has also an interest in the art and thought of the contemporary world, bringing to its interpretation judgment and experience enriched from the state of art in past epochs.[4]

But let us return to the problem of theology. In the fifteenth century there was a sense of antagonism between humanism in its early phase and theology, so much so that historians sometimes speak of a pagan revival. Paganism, however, soon dwindled.[5] The philosophy of Plato and

[4] Teaching the practice of any of the fine arts is a special problem in American education, which will be discussed later. The theory of the fine arts is sometimes fused with the practice of them and sometimes separated from practice.

[5] Paganism never quite disappears. In the nineteenth century, for instance, the outlooks of poets like Heinrich Heine and Algernon Charles Swinburne, and in the twentieth century the attempt of the Nazis to substitute Germanic myth for Christianity are examples of this. An interesting study of a characteristic phase of this eternal recurrence of paganism is *The Tyranny of Greece over Germany* by E. M. Butler, most easily available as a Beacon Press paperback, Boston, 1958. The book originally was published by Macmillan in 1935.

his successors had profoundly affected the development of Christian thought in earlier centuries. Why should the re-interpretation of Greek thought in the Renaissance now imply an attack upon Christianity? The aims of humanism and of Christianity were in many respects identical. Could not the better parts of the classical tradition, without too much distortion, be interpreted from a Christian point of view? Accordingly, Christian philosophers and Christian teachers arose to harmonize the interests of ancient ideal-ism and Christian idealism, a work notably carried for-ward in the teaching of Greek and Latin by the Jesuits in seventeenth-century Europe. The product was—and is—known as Christian humanism. This does not mean that all Christians are humanists or that all humanists are Christians, but it throws light on the relation of the hu-manities in modern times to theology. In American educa-tion, courses in "religion" are commonly classed with the humanities, whereas, as we have noted, courses in theology are commonly assigned to the divinity school.[6] In this latter sense theology is technical. In the broader sense theology as a group of religious ideas concerning the na-ture of man strongly influences contemporary humanism.

If earlier tensions between theology and humanism have thus diminished, it should also be noticed that the study of science and of the social sciences is not per se to be counted "inhumane," even though incautious humanists occasionally seem to say so. A humane scientist is not a contradiction in terms, and, obviously, a specialist in one of the humanities may turn out to be a selfish, self-cen-tered gossip whose tongue is a terror to the community. There is nothing in the nature of the social sciences, more-

[6] Another excellent book, dealing with the transition from ancient cul-ture to Christian culture, is Charles Norris Cochrane's *Christianity and Classical Culture: A Study of Thought and Action from Augustus to Augustine*. This was originally published by Oxford University Press in 1940, but is now most easily available as one of the Galaxy Books, 1957.

over, to inhibit the development of a broad, generous, and philosophic interpretation of man in society.

Nevertheless, across the years and in many civilizations (for example, that of ancient China) the experience of the race seems to show that certain kinds of knowledge, faithfully pursued, do help to elevate the spirit and refine the sensibilities of those who study them. He who profits by these studies becomes humane; that is, his sympathies are awakened for what is excellent and averted from what is evil. Through the sympathetic interpretation of cultures other than his own, and of the arts and philosophies that have shaped or been born into these cultures and of the better parts of his own, he can grow more mature, more sensitive, more generous in mind and spirit at the same time that he becomes better informed. He learns more about the potentialities for good and evil in human life and thought. Such, at least, is the theory of humanism; and since over the centuries a sufficient number of human beings have shaped their lives in the light of this theory, American colleges and universities persist in offering instruction in the humanities.[7] It is of course impossible to make a silk purse out of a sow's ear. Many persons in college do not deserve to be there, and so it sometimes happens that exposure to the humanities does not have the desired effect upon undergraduates. But just as the occasional inability of high-school pupils to grasp algebra is not an adequate reason for abandoning the teaching of mathematics, so the failure of humane studies to "do anything" to this or that undergraduate is no reason for abandoning or abolishing them.

[7] Because for many decades these studies were principally the property of an upper-class minority, they were sometimes referred to as "polite learning" or "polite letters." This definition lingers in dictionaries. The alteration of the class structure in modern times renders this meaning obsolete and makes the interpretation unjust to the potentialities latent in the contemporary humanities. If "polite" be generously construed, however, the statement still makes sense.

The humanities are, then, a group of subjects devoted to the study of man as a being other than a biological product and different from a social or sociological entity.[8] They make certain assumptions about human nature and about history. First, they assume that man lives in a dimension lying beyond science and the social sciences. Second, they assume that his profound sense of individuation is one of the most important things about him. Third, they assume that the better traits of humanity, or, if one likes, the enduring elements of human nature, find typical expression in philosophy, in literature, in language, and in the arts, and that history is both the way by which these expressions are preserved and one of the principal modes of interpreting the meaning of these expressions to and in contemporary life. Historically, since they sprang from ancient Greece and Rome, humane studies antecede theology and are not primarily conditioned by theological considerations, but like theology they aim at a better state of being for man. Fourth, the purpose of the humanities is refining and maturing the individual who studies them sympathetically and intelligently, evidence of refinement and maturation being given by increased sympathy with and understanding of philosophy and the arts in past and present time and increased sympathy with and understanding of man not only as he is but as he has been. Humane studies tend to concentrate upon individual development rather more than upon social judgment, and differ from science in this regard also, since science properly seeks to eliminate the personal equation. Incidental to these several aims, humane learning also creates, as it were, methods and disciplines of its own, such as intellectual history.

[8] See in this connection *The Absurdity of Christianity and Other Essays* by Archibald Allan Bowman, edited by Charles W. Hendel, The Liberal Arts Press, 1958.

4

Probably there never was a time in the history of the Western world when the humanities, however defined, included all the branches of knowledge. Old-line humanists, proud of a great tradition of learning that not only rediscovered the radiant universe of antiquity but also restored dignity to human nature, have been perturbed as they have been forced to watch whole provinces of their intellectual empire set up as independent kingdoms. Thus science has ceased to be "natural philosophy" and the social sciences are no longer content to remain under the tent of "political science" or "political philosophy." The overwhelming increase of specialized information in all branches of knowledge makes it increasingly impossible for anybody to regain the concept of unity of knowledge possible even as late as the mid-nineteenth century.[9] On the other hand, the need for understanding what knowledge is all about and why man pursues it is a philosophic problem that, if it concerns science and the social sciences, deeply concerns the humanities by virtue of being philosophic. Being philosophic, humane learning, though it cannot unify knowledge, can at least help preserve the ideal aim of knowledge. Education in the humanities only, given the present state of the world, would be quite as

[9] Among various attempts to find unity in diversity the volume entitled *The Unity of Knowledge* (Doubleday, 1955), edited by Lewis Leary and comprising papers delivered at one of the Bicentennial Conferences of Columbia University, is characteristic. The editor concludes: "As we talked, the bold concept of a unity of knowledge became modified to something . . . more manageable. . . . What agreement emerged looked not so much toward unity as toward a federated union in which different types of orientation toward knowledge are not simply juxtaposed . . . but are differentiated in function, method, and content in relation to a large universe of orientation to the world and to society." This is gallant, but as one of the participants said, we must still "look for a focus which our civilization perhaps lacks."

narrow or one-sided as education only in the sciences or only in the social sciences. The humanities have no monopoly on educational virtue, but they can and do maintain a noble educational end: keeping in view the ways by which individuals can be led to maturity through the development of intelligence and the refinement of sensibility. They are a storehouse of wisdom, beauty, and experience, but they are not the only such storehouse. The humane person is not merely the product of the humanities, but he is a person who, recognizing the great intent of humane learning, strives to keep his own learning, be it scientific, social, or humanistic, truly humane.

TWO

The Humanities As Information

We have, it is hoped, clarified the relations among the three great categories of knowledge, and discussed some of the fundamental concepts concerning the humanities. It is now time to turn to another of the leading questions asked by our businessman and to try to answer it in some detail. That question is "Why is it that you think the humanities are so important?" Let us examine this issue in terms of American life today, and let us begin as simply as we can. Let us begin with the humanities as sources of useful information—or, for that matter, desirable information, whether immediately useful or not.

Americans have developed an enormous respect for exact knowledge. This is evident in the vogue of crossword puzzles and other word games, in the renewed popularity of spelling matches on the radio, and in the demand of business for "better"—that is, for grammatically more exacting—English. Another instance is the vogue of radio and television shows of the "Information Please" variety. When these take the form of stumping the experts, listeners look up disputed points in their reference books if there is argument among the panel, and hotly telephone or write the broadcasting station. The same degree of exactitude is demanded of the quiz show that gives money away. Not only is the United States the first nation of modern times to turn the acquisition of accurate (and often out-of-the-way) information into a national game, it is also the first to pay out hundreds of thousands of dollars every year to the contestants. Equally striking is the fact that this display of knowledge is entirely useless; *i.e.,* the correct identification of the ingredients of French recipes does not send the housewife to the cookstove, nor does a list of operatic heroines successfully recited add to the number of American opera companies.

Characteristic also is the wide vogue among us of dictionaries, encyclopedias, books of reference, handbooks, guides, almanacs, and annuals. Ignoring the ancient doctrine that there is no royal road to learning, Americans apparently feel that there ought to be a democratic one, and publishers obligingly try to pave this with reference works. These are advertised as having two particular merits: they "save time," and they are by the "latest authorities" and therefore contain the newest word. Obsolescence is inevitable in all reference books, but what is illuminating here is the implication of accuracy. The latest authorities obviously give you the latest word, and the latest word is supposed to be the exact word. Undoubtedly there are immensely useful handbooks in all fields, but it is nevertheless true that for general consumption these publications concern the area of humane learning more richly than they do the exact sciences and quite as much as they do the social sciences. This is due in part to the fact that the language of science is not understandable by the layman in the same degree as is the language of history or of the arts.

Across the centuries and over the world humanistic learning has accumulated an immense amount of information about mankind and its actions. This information steadily increases in amount, range, and accuracy with the passing years—hence, the appeal of the "latest authorities."

Waiving every other consideration for the moment, one may reasonably claim for the compiler of information in the field of the humanities the same social function that is allotted the compiler of any other form of information, from baseball scores to birds of the Bible. To know something and to know it accurately is usually accounted a praiseworthy thing. Americans respect accurate information, and the humanistic scholar gives it to them. The argument may seem naïve, but as critics of the humanities sometimes write or speak as if acquiring exact information in this area were an odd thing to do, one can only retort that without the activity of such scholars about one third of our available information about man would, in the first place, in growing more and more obsolescent, grow more and more untrustworthy, and, in the second place, would eventually disappear.

Because we take reference books for granted, we do not comprehend how much gray matter goes into their making. Let us examine one of the commonest reference books —the dictionary. An English dictionary is our common guide to the meaning, spelling, and use of words. Few of its users realize that a dictionary is like an iceberg, seven-eighths of it out of sight. Few understand what an amazing amount of patient scholarly work has had to be done, and still must be done, to create an accurate dictionary. There was no dictionary of English until just before the discovery of America. About 1440 a Norfolk Dominican monk named Galfridus Grammaticus compiled a small list of words with definitions in Latin, for schoolboys (hence, *Promptorium Parvulorum*). This was published in 1499. Not until 1730, however, when Nicholas Bailey brought out a dictionary supposed to contain words "in good usage," did any dictionary of English pretend to be general; and not until 1857, when Archbishop Richard Chenevix Trench in a celebrated paper laid down the rule that a dictionary should record the actual language and not merely the preferences or prejudices of its maker, was the basis of a modern scientific dictionary made clear to the English-speaking peoples.

If we look into a good unabridged dictionary—Webster's will do—we can begin to understand the importance of humanistic scholarship in the matter of securing accurate information. Here, as an example, are the entries under a word that presently concerns us—the word *human:*

hu′man (hū′măn), *adj.* [OF. *humain,* fr. L. *humanus;* akin to L. *homo* man. See HOMAGE; cf. HUMANE, 2d OMBER.] 1. Belonging or relating to man; characteristic of man; as, *human* lineaments, nature, frailties.

2. Designating, or being, a man; consisting of men; having human form or attributes; as, the *human* race.

3. Characteristic of, or relating to, man in his essential nature as distinguished from the nonhuman; specif.: **a** Of, pertaining to, or resembling, man or his attributes, in distinction from the lower animal world; as, the dog displayed *human* intelligence. **b** Of or relating to man as distinguished from the superhuman or the extrahuman, from the divine, or from nature; belonging to finite intelligence and powers.

> To err is *human;* to forgive, divine.   *Pope.*

c Susceptible to or representative of the sympathies and frailties of man's nature; as, statesmen who are *human.*

4. Of or pert. to the social life, or the collective relations, of mankind; as, *human* institutions; *human* progress.

5. = HUMANE.

6. *Astrol.* Symbolized or figured by a human being; as, the *human* signs (Gemini, Virgo, Sagittarius, and Aquarius).

Syn. — HUMAN, HUMANE, MORTAL. HUMAN applies to whatever is characteristic of man as man; it frequently connotes, esp. in modern usage, the common sympathies, passions, or failings of men, often in implied contrast with an attitude of superiority to them; as, "brutish forms, rather than *human*" (*Milton*); "if powers divine behold our *human* actions" (*Shak.*); "Yet tears to *human* suffering are due"

(*Wordsworth*). HUMANE (still sometimes applied broadly to whatever is befitting or honorable to humanity or which tends to humanize or refine) commonly refers, in modern usage, to that which evinces active sympathy or compassion for other human beings, or (esp.) for the lower animals; as, "Shakespeare or Vergil — souls in whom sweetness and light, and all that in *human* nature is most *humane,* were eminent" (*M. Arnold*); *humane* studies; "Ah, treat [thy horses] kindly! . . . show that thou hast mercy, which the great, with needless hurry whirled from place to place, *humane* as they would seem, not always show" (*Cowper*); the *Humane* Society. MORTAL, as here compared (cf. DEADLY), emphasizes more strongly than *human* the idea of transiency, limitation, or frailty, and (often) suggests a contrast with *immortal;* as, "invisible to *mortal* sight" (*Milton*); "our *mortal* nature's strife" (*Shelley*); "her stature more than *mortal*" (*Tennyson*); cf. "looking . . . larger than *human*" (*id.*).

hu′man (hū′măn), *n.* A human being, esp. as a species of creature. "Sprung of *humans* that inhabit earth." *Chapman.*

If all we want of a dictionary is pronunciation and spelling, this massive entry will not interest us. But if (as in the case of *human, humane, humanism,* the *humanities,* and *humanistic*) differences among the meanings of like terms and differences among the meanings of a single term become a matter of importance (lawsuits and business contracts sometimes turn on such issues), what a wealth of information is here made crystal clear! We learn how the word originated, and with what words it is connected, and some dictionaries will also give the date on which the word (or the words) first appeared in manuscript or print. We sort out six separate meanings of the adjective, and learn another one for the noun. We have a compact little essay that really tells us about three words that are sometimes synonyms and sometimes not, carefully distinguishing the synonymous meaning from other meanings in each case, and illustrating each phase of meaning by a passage from a notable writer. How long would it take the untrained person merely to read Chapman, Pope, Milton, Wordsworth, Shakespeare, Arnold, Cowper, Shelley, and Tennyson in order to hunt down relevant passages containing the words *human, humane,* and *mortal?* How long would it take him to phrase these careful definitions and distinctions of meaning, including the (to most of us) unexpected reference to four signs of the zodiac under meaning six? Which of us, offhand, would relate *human* to *homage,* or, of all strange connections, to *omber,* a game of cards? Yet this is only one entry in one column of one page of a book, 2,987 pages of which, each carrying three columns of similar entries, constitute the dictionary. What immense learning is here usefully deployed! [1] Just as the labors of thousands of chemists, some of them famous, some of them now unknown, are buried, so to speak, in the bit of plastic on the table or in a new lifesaving drug, so the labors of thousands of scholars, stretching back to Sanskrit grammarians who lived centuries before Christ, are concealed in the dictionary we so casually consult and put aside.[2] Communication between men and among nations is, we are told, one of the leading problems of the world. It is therefore an important duty of American culture to see that linguistic studies continue. If every great nation must have a "concern" for the richness, exactitude, range, and depth in time of the language it speaks, every great nation must, to achieve this aim, have an equal concern for other languages and for linguistic science as a whole.

[1] Cyprus is very much in the public eye. Again to illustrate the wealth of scholarship easily available to anybody, let the candid reader go to any good encyclopedia—the *Britannica* will serve—and study for a few minutes the enormous amount of information condensed into usable form in the article on that historic island. He will learn, if he learns nothing else, how complex the cultural history of Cyprus has been.

[2] The complexities of linguistic science are brilliantly set forth in Leonard Bloomfield, *Language,* Holt, 1933.

2

Americans have an abiding interest in history and historical traditions. This is evident in their roadside signs, in the preservation or restoration of places like Williamsburg, Old Sturbridge, and Virginia City, in the requirement (sometimes foolish) of courses in American history in the public schools and in state-supported institutions of higher learning, in the popularity of historical pageants like Paul Green's *The Lost Colony,* in the vogue of historical romances such as *Gone With the Wind,* and in an almost religious reverence for historical figures like Washington, Lincoln, and Lee and for historical documents such as the Declaration of Independence and the Constitution of the United States. It also appears in the vogue of genealogical societies. Most states have their official historical societies; and the American Historical Association is chartered by the Congress of the United States. In some ways, indeed, it seems probable that the study of history is more readily accepted as a normal human occupation than is the pursuit of other branches of humane learning.

This interest in history is no recent development. It began with the coming of the English to the New World. Captain John Smith was convinced he had a historical mission to perform, the New England Puritans were persuaded that God had sifted a nation to inaugurate a new phase of history in North America, and when Bishop George Berkeley wrote his celebrated line "Westward the course of empire takes its way," he was phrasing a common belief. The antebellum South sometimes thought of itself as a modernized version of Greek democracy, the nation entered World War I to fulfill its historic mission of making the world safe for democracy, and today, in the period of the cold war, Americans continue to believe that history has made them the chief guardians and proponents of democracy. Their historic duty is through military alliances, economic aid, and cultural institutes, to spread democracy abroad. We even talk sometimes of an "American century," and our historians, from George Bancroft to Frederick Jackson Turner, have done what they could to analyze the unique historical mission or quality or component of development of the United States.

Like some of the other general terms that have appeared in this discussion, "history" is a noun of rich and complicated meaning. For most Americans it calls up memories of a high-school or college class in history and of the textbooks one had to secure for such a course. There is, therefore, a natural tendency to suppose that the chief duty of a historian is to write a textbook. Moreover, despite what has just been said about American historical interest, it is probable that most adults do not again read history books, though an occasional newspaper story, magazine article, television show, campaign speech, or popular historical novel may call up fragmentary memories of what they learned in "history." [3] But the apparent contradiction between this lack of a continuing reading interest in history and the claim that there is a traditional and pervasive American belief in historical learning and in the historical process need not disturb us. Instead, let us distinguish between formal historical works and the feeling, vague though it may be, for a historical point of view. The distinction is important, for it throws light on the question, already touched on, whether history belongs with the social sciences or with the humanities. So far as a historian is a professional technician, he operates scientifically and belongs with the social sciences. So far as he is a literary

---

[3] A minority of persons outside the academic world continues to take pleasure in books on historical subjects, including biography and such philosophic studies of history as that of Toynbee.

artist (and great historians from Herodotus to Henry Adams were literary artists) and, even more important, so far as he expresses, even unconsciously, a general philosophic point of view, he may, without injustice to science, be classed with the humanities. As Dr. Boyd C. Shafer, secretary of the American Historical Association, has said: "History is a search into the whole of man's life on earth, a search to find out how man developed and how he became what he is." Dr. Shafer added, partly paraphrasing a famous Latin sentence about history, "History is the memory of man. Without a knowledge of it, he would be lost, just as a man would be with amnesia—without his memory."

Now the American instinct for history, which is a deeper thing than the question of how many history books Americans read, is a sound instinct, one that relates both their culture and their development to a central component of Western humanism. This component is the historical sense; that is, the feeling both of and for history as an active agent shaping human destiny. So essential is the historical sense to the understanding of Western development that it is sometimes called the special attribute marking off the culture of the Atlantic community[4] from the other great cultures of the world. Two of the leading civilizations of the East—those of India and China—are

[4] This awkward phrase reveals a genuine difficulty. To talk about "Western" culture is in the minds of many to exclude Russia from the West, even though Marxism is a development from Western philosophic thought brought about by a German working in the British Museum. To talk of "European" culture seems to exclude the United States, albeit the phrase would be sympathetically received throughout Latin America. The "Atlantic community" at least includes both sides of that ocean, but it is really not accurate, since our culture began in the eastern Mediterranean and was strongly influenced by cultures existing along the Nile, in the Tigris-Euphrates valleys, and, supremely in the area of morality, by the culture of Asia Minor, including Palestine. What is intended is that large fraction of mankind whose culture has been shaped by the fusion of Greek thought, Roman law, and Christianity that lies at the basis of the "modern world."

said to have been until recent times relatively unhistorical in outlook, and much the same thing has been said of Japan. The inhabitants of the Dark Continent (Egypt must be excepted) for the most part have exhibited small historical sense, nor did the original Australians and the Polynesians have any. If the Saracens developed historical scholarship, it is supposed this came through their contacts with the Western world by way of Byzantium. Moreover, the pessimistic religions of the ancient East placed little value on history for the reason that, in their systems of thought, life is illusion and the business of the sage is first to endure it and second to escape from it. An idea like that of social development, an idea like that of progress were alien to such religions. They made no sense. But in the Western tradition, as the Italian scholar Norberto Bobbio put it, man is a historical being, he is a being in history, and he makes history. The American version of this philosophical remark is in some sense Abraham Lincoln's famous saying "We cannot escape history."

To most of us the image of a historian is that of a man poring over the provisions of a treaty or the records of a military campaign. Public policy and public documents will always furnish an important part of the materials of history, and in the nineteenth century history was once defined as past politics. But in the twentieth century both the field and the concept of history have enormously widened. Written or printed documents no longer suffice. Ancient monuments with or without inscriptions, fragments of pottery,[5] old coins, wall paintings, and even

[5] One of the most erudite of learned publications, begun in 1919, is the *Corpus Vasorum Antiquorum*, published with the co-operation of scholars in fourteen nations under the auspices of the International Academic Union, of which the American Council of Learned Societies is a member. This series is confined to Greek pottery with painted decoration. Why? Said Edmond Pottier, who invented the project, "The painting on pottery is, with literature, the richest source of our knowledge about all the various aspects of life in Antiquity and the feeling of the Greek's soul,

human bones and the fragments of former life buried in the grave are now drawn upon as historical sources to help us answer the question of how man developed and how he became what he is. Of the twenty-nine societies concerned with humanistic learning and making up the American Council of Learned Societies, there is not one but has an important historical interest, and most of them are, in the broad philosophic sense, committed to the historical point of view, that is, to a historical interpretation of human life, art, thought, philosophy, and culture. It would seem, then, that humanistic scholarship, far from being remote in the eyes of Americans, is at the very center of the national feeling for the meaning of American development, a feeling that links the United States with the cultural traditions of the general Atlantic community. That most characteristic part of the American credo, our belief in progress, commits us to history. How can we know how far we have come unless we discover where and what we have been?

3

Partly as a result of history, Americans find themselves in a cold war, that is, they live in a state of continuing political, military, and cultural tension vis-à-vis a power quite as strong as the United States. This is a new and unpleasant experience, one, furthermore, that seems to be without any foreseeable end. So far as the military aspect of the struggle is concerned, despite occasional flurries of doubt, and thanks to brilliant work by science, industry, and the national government, Americans seem to be doing pretty well. Diplomacy has built up a series of interlocking

and at the same time the most spontaneous and varied revelation of their artistic genius." Thus it is that history broadens. *Bulletin 1954–1955 of the International Council for Philosophy and Humanistic Studies (C.I.P.S.H.),* Paris, p. 37.

alliances through which they extend military aid to their allies; and though the wisdom of this policy is now and again challenged in reference to a particular nation, Americans are at least reconciled to the necessity of keeping up the system. In a cynical view a military alliance may be said to be no better than its weakest link, but at least the Russians hold us in healthy respect, and in a general way the spread of communism has been checked.

When, however, attention shifts to economic aid, bewilderment and contradiction appear. Sending American men, money, and machinery abroad does not automatically produce either friendship or democracy. Aid of this sort seems ever and again to move one country in the direction of socialism, another in the direction of totalitarianism, and a third in no ascertainable direction at all, certainly not in the direction of the democratic ideal of a better life for everybody. Representatives of the United States abroad, working on their lawful occasions, have even been set upon, imprisoned, or deported as enemies of the country the Americans were trying to help; and well-meant programs of agricultural know-how, medical aid, educational enlightenment, and so on have been assaulted as disguised colonialism, "Americanization" in an unwelcome sense, materialism, and moral hypocrisy. Why are we so often misunderstood?

Or is it that we do not always take the trouble to try to understand the foreign country concerned, and therefore blunderingly and unwittingly arouse suspicion and antagonism? Obviously, sending gang plows to a nation whose arable land is held by peasants in one-, two-, three-, four-, or five-acre plots not only fails to help the peasant but leads to an understandable charge of appalling ignorance on the part of the United States. One of the tenets of American democracy is the duty of every individual to better himself, but this ideal does not automatically appeal to the inhabitants of a land whose dominant system of thought has been for centuries the duty of submission to the will of God. The American industrial order assumes as a matter of course that workers will present themselves at regular times for regular jobs for regular wages, but an American mission, full of altruistic zeal for a backward territory, has on occasion been baffled to discover that the "natives" were not in the least interested in this pattern of life, worked when they felt like it, quit when they wanted to, and could not understand a concept like that of "incentive pay." A country content for centuries to leave the management of its economic and social policies to a small elite class is not overnight easily going to accept our notion of government by majority. An easy way out is to fall back into the nineteenth-century habit of regarding these odd people as benighted, but this, however flattering to the American ego, does nothing for international understanding, American defense, or the containment of communism.

Anthropologists, sociologists, and economists who have special knowledge of this or that undeveloped area can of course help the American government and American business to overcome such provincialism, and have often succeeded in doing so. But social scientists are among the first to declare that they do not pretend to know the whole truth about other cultures. The traditions, the art, the philosophy, the religion, the moral system, and the history of the peoples living in areas abroad need also to be sympathetically explored; and the languages spoken in other lands must be mastered by those who are going out to deal face to face with their inhabitants.[6] But it is precisely in these departments of learning that humanistic scholarship is important, no less than scholarship in the

[6] During the war years there were created what became known as "area and language studies," that is, programs concerning a specific nation or people which combined information relevant to the area from the social sciences and from the humanities.

social sciences. When relevant information of this kind is neglected, things can go very wrong indeed.

Here are warning examples from history. In the days when India was governed by the British, the British, with the best intentions in the world, tried to impose Anglo-Saxon notions of law, including the conduct of courts, upon the multifarious peoples of that enormous subcontinent. But so primary an idea as that of justice means one thing to a Parsi, another thing to a Brahman, a third to a Moslem, a fourth to a Buddhist, and something else to other cultural and religious groups, however much they all believe in justice in the abstract. So, likewise, concepts of a fair trial, the credibility of witnesses, the rights of the defendant, the function of the judge, and the nature of an appropriate punishment for wrongdoing vary widely from those found among the British. Desirable though it was to end "anarchy" by imposing a single legal system, the attempt created confusion, heartburning, resentment, and hatred as frequently as it advanced the cause of order.[7] Again: If in 1857 British military authorities at home and in Bengal had known more than they apparently knew about the religious beliefs of their sepoy troops, the occasion of the Indian mutiny might not have occurred. The cartridges for the new European rifles were covered by grease at one end, and the soldier was supposed to bite off the greased paper before the cartridge could be fired. The sepoys were told that the grease was the grease of pigs and cows, and was thus unclean to both Moslems and Hindus, and no amount of tardy explanation could alter this belief. Forced to obey orders, they mutinied, and the cruelty they practised was in part due to their sense of religious out-

[7] The caution with which the government of Israel is working out a unitary system of law and of legal procedure amid the complexities of Mosaic law, Talmudic law, Turkish law, Mohammedan custom, British mandate law, the customary law of the Bedouins, and so forth is revealing in this connection.

rage. We who, by Supreme Court decision, permit a religious sect like Jehovah's Witnesses to follow their peculiar customs in the refusal because of religious scruples to salute the American flag ought to be careful to listen to humanists and social scientists when they speak of the odd beliefs of other peoples—odd, perhaps, to us, but usually explicable in terms of the history, custom, philosophical outlook, and religious values of the cultures involved.

Here is another illuminating lesson in understandable differences between East and West of the kind that may help or hinder us in the cold war. Our museums contain a good many examples of Asian sculpture. It does not take a great deal of observation by the layman, if he compares the treatment of the human body in Hindu and Chinese sculpture with that in the sculpture of the West, to note that from the Greeks to Epstein, Western artists delight in displaying their knowledge of anatomy, whereas the artists of India and China seem indifferent to anatomical and muscular correctness. This is sometimes interpreted to mean that the Asian artist was backward, or deficient, or unable to solve the problem.

But was he? The Chinese craftsmen who carved the wonderful jade and ivory objects that also adorn the museums, the artisans who decorated the temples of India with intricate stone carvings as delicate as lace, the sculptors who created statues of Buddha that are among the masterpieces of world art can scarcely be accused of lack of skill. There comes now a competent humanistic scholar, a historian of art, to solve the puzzle. Placing, as it were, pairs of analogous statues, one in the tradition of Hellenism and one in the tradition of Orientalism, side by side, he makes clear what should have been evident all along, except that the rest of us did not have the necessary aesthetic insight and scholarly information. Western man, entranced by his own image, finds the human body a beautiful object in and of itself. He therefore studies it, he idealizes it, he shapes a perfect image of it on athletic models, as in the case of the Laocoön or the Apollo Belvedere. The aim of the Oriental sculptor was not an athletic but a spiritual perfection, his canons of proportion were mathematical, not physiological, and his desire was not to idealize the body but to surpass it, to make it the occasion of a lesson in ethical behavior by withdrawing man from earthly distractions. Not the perfection of mortality, but an impression of more than mortal life is what he aimed at. His sculpture suggests, in the words of a student of Indian philosophy, a supraterrestrial unearthly substance. The ideal of the one culture is activity, of the other, repose; the one seeks to express the muscular energy we Americans admire in boxers, trackmen, football players, and swimmers; the other expresses timeless serenity, the passionless calm possible to the saintly and the wise.[8] And before, Philistine-like, we dismiss this distinction as of interest only to specialists in art history, think of the opposite attitudes toward things like social work, athletic contests, economic competition, and the gospel of getting on in the world that flow from the two opposed philosophies of what man is here on earth to do. There is a half-truth in the adage: "Tell me what you eat and I will tell you what you are," but there is profounder political and social truth in the warning: "Tell me what your values are before I try to alter your economic system."

When international tension degenerates into total war, as it did in World War II, and threatened to do in the case of the Korean conflict, the relevance of information available to the nation through humanistic scholarship can become startlingly clear. When, some time before Pearl

[8] See Benjamin Rowland, *Art in East and West*, Harvard University Press, 1955, pp. 8 ff. The phrase about unearthly substance Mr. Rowland quotes from H. Zimmer's *Philosophies of India*, Pantheon Books, 1951.

Harbor, the American Council of Learned Societies, largely through the instigation of its then administrative secretary, Mortimer Graves, and with funds from the Rockefeller Foundation, launched what came to be known as the Intensive Language Program, very little attention was paid to this innovation by the world of practical affairs. A goodly amount of the interest of Mr. Graves had gone into what came to be known as the "funny languages"—the minor dialects of Asia, Polynesia, and so on. It was at the time almost impossible to study Thai (Siamese), Malay, Korean, and like tongues and dialects in the United States, for there were few or no textbooks or dictionaries or reading material, phonograph recordings, or grammars. The first effort of the program was therefore devoted to producing teaching materials at a time when such activities looked like the idlest of scholarly interests. The second effort of the program was to develop ways and means of learning these, and other, languages rapidly. Then came Pearl Harbor, the loss of the Philippines, and the momentary triumph of Japan, and suddenly information about these same "funny languages" became more than pertinent, it became an essential part of winning the war. Let Mr. Graves tell the story:

. . . it was necessary immediately to move over into teaching these Asian languages rather than merely producing materials for instruction. 1942 consequently was a year in which the Intensive Language Program developed language instruction in languages not normally available in American curricula in accordance with the following principles, which, if not entirely new, were new in this combination: 1) intensive use of time; 2) incessant drill by native speakers; 3) control by trained linguistic scientists . . . ; 4) new materials designed for use in this context; 5) small classes. . . . When the U.S. Army took up the problem of teaching languages to troops and to officers, the Intensive Language Program was ready for it. For the next two years, consequently, the ACLS-Army cooperative effort resulted—in the activities of the Language and Area Courses of the Army Specialized Training Program, the Civil Affairs Training Schools of the Provost Marshal General's Office, and the Language Branch of the U.S. Armed Forces Institute—in an immense amount of instruction in accordance with the new combination of principles and the production of teaching materials of one kind or another in about fifty languages. Twenty-six textbooks with accompanying teacher's manuals and records and four dictionaries were published by the ACLS first for the Army and then for public distribution. . . .[9]

Yet, despite this sound lesson in the relevance of humanistic disciplines to a war effort in the twentieth century, when the Korean conflict broke out information about the Korean language was hard to find. Why?

In 1919 Korean was a forbidden language, and information about it was scarce. In Korea, however, a group of devoted scholars joined together in a small and hidden office in Seoul, determined to create a definitive and complete dictionary of the Korean language. Without funds and at the risk of imprisonment they labored for twenty-six years, until the Japanese departed in 1945. Rockefeller Foundation funds were then made available, work on the text was virtually completed, and printing actually begun in 1950—when the Korean War erupted, printing plants were seized, the manuscripts were dispersed, and the whole project apparently was killed forever. As soon, however, as the armistice was signed, these same scholars went back to work, dug out the hidden manuscripts, repaired and completed them, and with paper supplied by the Foundation, again began to print. The dictionary is now complete, in six large volumes, a monument not only to humanistic scholarship in general, but to Korean courage, patriotism, and devotion to one's cultural heritage. Some of these scholars were old men of seventy-five and eighty.

[9] *Thoughts on the Humanities by Some Officers of the American Council of Learned Societies,* Washington, January 20, 1955.

It is, however, not merely in times of war that a knowledge of appropriate foreign languages is desirable. The Continental businessman, if he is a leading banker, industrialist, wholesaler, or other person engaged in more than local trade (and, for that matter, the retailer also) knows more than one language as a matter of course. He masters a second language (and sometimes a third and fourth) not merely to talk to tourists, but because, as the concept of Pan-Europe grows, as history throws him more and more into contact with nationals from other continents in matters like trade, concessions, raw materials, and so on, he finds he cannot carry out his export policies in terms of his native speech. Why should the American business leader, likewise thrown into contact with leading men in other countries, handicap himself by linguistic isolation? Why should the American ambassador or the American consul have to operate through an interpreter? Being ignorant of the country to which he is accredited because he is ignorant of the language and literature of that country does not seem to make for good diplomatic relations, and, *pari passu,* the same thing is true of that other form of diplomacy, international business. Of course, the European, or Latin American, or Asian probably speaks English, but the fact that English is a secondary tongue abroad does not obviate the necessity of a second tongue at home. So patent is the absurdity of linguistic isolation that our State Department has set up a Foreign Language Institute for the training of personnel in all ranks from ambassador to stenographer, in the language and customs of the country to which the American is going. In the words of Professor Henri Peyre of Yale University:

[The] history of the last fifty years in several countries has proved conclusively that statesmen who had been trained as engineers, as scientists, even as military or business men, have regularly failed when they attempted to lead men and to deal with human affairs, in which irrational and unpredictable factors predominate. We have ourselves heard physicians, lawyers and politicians declare that no one should attempt to get into politics who has not mastered one art or one foreign literature. British papers have more than once remarked since 1950 that the root of many British troubles in the Middle East and the Near East, and the root of similar mistakes now being committed by the Americans lay in their narrow quantitative approach to problems which cannot be thus solved. A little curiosity for Iranian traditions as embodied in literature, or for the literary and cultural heritage of the Greeks, the Italians, the French, would have gone a long way in appealing to the emotional forces which far more than economic necessity, impel these peoples to behave sentimentally, illogically, proudly.[10]

4

Here, then, are three links between the ordinary interests of average Americans of some education and responsibility as citizens, and the kind of information the humanities, humanistic teaching, and humanistic scholarship have to offer. 1) The humanities and humanistic scholarship maintain a great library of information kept perpetually up to date. 2) Humanistic scholarship maintains (and maintains almost singlehanded) all the knowledge of history we have. 3) The humanities and humane learning are one of the principal ways by which we can sympathetically approach and maintain friendly relations with other countries, and, lacking cultural and linguistic information, our business and our foreign policy alike suffer from our own self-imposed ignorance.

As Dean Theodore C. Blegen of the University of Minnesota writes: "Consider the role of the humanities in

[10] Henri Peyre, *The Need for Language Study in America Today*, The Cultural Division of the French Embassy, 972 Fifth Avenue, New York, 1954, p. 40.

helping to answer major questions centering in the meeting of minds in a world made small by invention but ever complex in its diversities of culture and language and tradition. . . . The many differences that trouble world relations touch the heart of humanistic studies, for they have to do not just with power and economics but also with religion, history, ideologies, traditions, literature, communication, the arts." [11]

[11] Theodore C. Blegen, "The Prospect for the Liberal Arts," *The Quarterly Journal of Speech,* XL (4), December, 1954, as quoted in *Thoughts on the Humanities.*

THREE

The Humanities and the Individual

We have discussed the utility, or at any rate the relevance, in American terms of the kinds of information humane learning has to give, choosing for analysis three representative areas of national interest. But our business-man asks another set of questions: What can the humanities do for me? For my family? For my business? For my community? Inasmuch as there is a sense in which business and the community exist only for the satisfaction of the individuals who compose the one and profit by the other, and since, clearly, in asking what the humanities can do for his family, the questioner thinks of his family as a set of persons, each having his own desires and talents, we may fairly reduce these several questions to a single inquiry: What can the humanities do for the individual in the United States? And though an individual may be anybody from an infant to a senile old person, we may again fairly assume that our questioner has in mind any representative American of either sex who is adult or on the way to adult status in the community. This will rule out children, but include high-school pupils, college students, and adults in the "real" world of traffic and trade. Certainly from the days of Socrates to the address of Professor Whitney J. Oates to the Modern Language Association of America in

1957, it has been consistently assumed that the business of the humanities is with the maturation of individuals.

Whatever *individual, individuality,* and *individualism* may mean in other cultures, these words have traditional power in the United States. The democracy of which we boast refers to a theory of government but it refers also to a social pattern, a "way of life." The theoretical basis of this way of life is the assumptions made in the Declaration of Independence and the Constitution, assumptions consonant alike with Christianity and with eighteenth-century rationalism. The assumptions dictate that every human being is an end in himself. That is what makes men equal. Equality, however, is not only a spiritual equality but an ethical equality as well. Americans, therefore, do not believe that the accident of birth confines anybody to a social caste, be it serfdom or aristocracy; and that is why they got rid of slavery in the nineteenth century and want to get rid of segregation in the twentieth. No class, they believe, is superior to the law. Translated into economics, the doctrine means equal opportunity for all; that is, without denying that men differ in ability, it assumes that every individual is entitled to advance in his chosen path as opportunity and merit permit. Every position in government, business, and society is theoretically open to free competition among qualified persons, and may the best man win! Hence, in principle, Americans oppose monopoly, insist upon public education, deprecate intolerance, and desire everyone to express his opinion on public issues freely within the limits of fundamental law. Many Americans are intolerant, many have no worth-while opinions to express, some are ignorant, and not every American square peg is in a square hole, but such, nevertheless, is the traditional ideal of the United States. It works toward an open rather than a closed society, it substitutes achievement for class and caste, it lies behind and gives emphasis to such familiar phrases as "Everybody must live his own life," "your own integrity," "You go your way and I'll go mine," "Let's agree to differ," "individual initiative," and many more.

But a concept of individualism suitable to a weak agrarian republic of three million souls needs new definition and acquires extraordinary complexities in an industrial empire of over 175 million people. The citizen is now fifty-eight times more insignificant than he was in 1789. His feeling of helplessness, already remarked by de Tocqueville in 1835 as endemic in democracy, has formidably increased. That is why he does not vote in the numbers that he should. What possible control does he have over the course of politics, industry, finance, government, amusement, education, art, war and peace? "They" arrange these things, often to "their" profit. If he wishes in his tiny way to become an effective public force, whether for change or for resistance to change, he must join something bigger than he is—a labor union, the Rotary Club, the American Legion. Yet in fusing his small interest with that of thousands, he further reduces his individual being. Reproached by critics for tolerating monotony, demagoguery, conformity, mediocrity, corruption, he can only make a helpless gesture.

Education and industry have combined to see that he becomes and remains socially well adjusted, a process that begins in the kindergarten and continues into the world of business under the watchful care of the personnel office. He is, of course, "free." He is "free," for example, to write to the editor, since newspapers are sensitive to public opinion, but he observes that sensitivity to public opinion is sensitivity to circulation and advertising. The magazine he buys in the subway or his wife brings home from a chain store is always the same magazine—the same vacuously pretty girl on the cover, the same vapid fiction in-

side, the same "leading article," a "think piece" by somebody who has name value and who goes through the form
but not the substance of discussion. His books he gets from
a wire rack in the drugstore, but "they" mysteriously remove some and bring in others at unexpected intervals.
His choice of radio, or television, or the movies is, more
often than not, a choice between Tweedledum and
Tweedledee, but so is his choice of a car, of clothing, of
textbooks for his children, and of the food he consumes,
bought in sanitary containers in sanitary stores where sanitary music softly plays. He becomes a number system—his
street address, his telephone, his car license, his operator's
license, his plant license, his enrollment in Blue Cross, his
social-security card, his hotel credit card, his insurance
policy, the chance he took on the new Chevrolet down at
the Masonic Hall. He ceases to be a person and becomes a
digit. To some interpreters his plight is so ominous that
they sketch a faceless future for his offspring, as in the
Brave New World of Aldous Huxley, the *1984* of George
Orwell, the *Fahrenheit 451* of Ray Bradbury. How far all
this is removed from the rest of Miranda's cry

> O brave new world
> That has such people in't!

That was uttered only seven or eight years after Captain
John Smith came to Jamestown!

If the pressure of circumstance thus depersonalizes the
citizen, the Freudian view of man popular in America
shakes his being to its very core. The citizen is no longer
someone having judgment and rationality; he has become
a psychological case, one in an endless chain of cases. The
clear light of eighteenth-century right reason fades into
the murk of the libido, the inferiority complex, penis
envy, incest, sadism, masochism, and the theory of rationalization. The nineteenth century believed in character; the

twentieth century has a devouring curiosity about personality. Personality traits are made the subject of statistical inquiry, as if people had gone to the wrong clothing
stores and had to begin sorting out their ill-assorted gar-
ments. Such phrases as a "disturbed person," the "well-
adjusted (or badly adjusted) person," the "neurotic personality of our time," a "pleasant personality" [1] are the
terms in which we now categorize the political heirs of
Jefferson and Franklin. On the distaff side the vocabulary
is equally enlightening: burlesque shows feature "personality girls," fashion shops implore you to choose a lipstick
suited to your personality, and a charm school guarantees
to "bring out your personality," meaning that it will
teach you a cunning device that may be mistaken for
allure. If Uncle Sam has yielded to the Man of the Year,
the American goddess is no longer Columbia the Gem of
the Ocean, but Aphrodite, with clothes chosen from the
pages of *Mademoiselle,* and smelling of "My Sin."

A paradoxical result of this unequal struggle between
the individual and the mass is not that the individual
melts into the mass but that the individual confesses to
loneliness, weakness, failure. The evidence is the findings
of psychoanalysis and social workers, statements by the
poets, and the appearance of this theme in modern fiction
and in plays like *A Streetcar Named Desire* and *Death of a
Salesman.* Our masses, which make for gregariousness,
conflict, apparently, with our mobile society, which makes
for rootlessness. The breakdown of the family as a func-
tioning unit strips the individual of a sense of refuge near
at hand, and the uncertainties of the draft, the cold war,

[1] Nothing is more illuminating than an inquiry that sometimes appears
on questionnaires sent out concerning candidates for a teaching post: "Is
there anything in his personality that would interfere with his success as
a teacher?" Even when this is intended as a euphemism for homosexual
tendencies, it throws an odd light on the canons by which we estimate
people.

the hydrogen bomb, and the artificial satellite deepen the sense of being forlorn. Where an Emerson grandly pictured man facing the gods, they alone and he alone, the letters sent to "Advice for the Lovelorn" columns continually sound the note of fear—the fear of being left out or left behind. The modern American is apparently afraid of insecurity, whether financial, emotional, or psychological. He fears not being liked. He fears, as he struggles toward status, not merely that no one will extend a helping hand, but also that, since the game must be played according to the rules "they" lay down, "they" are watching for his slightest slip. In vain, to the admiration of American Browning societies, did the hero in "Childe Roland" dauntless set the slug-horn to his lips; the modern substitute is: "Don't stick your neck out." McCarthyism had something to do with this, but it preceded McCarthy.[2]

2

Obviously the American tradition of rugged individualism would be totally undermined were there not powerful counterforces at work. The Judaeo-Christian ethic is still powerful enough to nourish individualism by bringing home to the soul a sense of responsibility for act and choice. Neither the concept of righteousness nor the concept of redeeming grace can be swept aside as components of the American outlook, however much sociological analysts may tend to read the church in terms of social factors only. No one present at a mass, a communion service, the Lord's Supper, or an equivalent mystery but must realize that for hundreds of thousands of Americans the spirit during these rites stands naked before its Maker. So, too, the legal concept of individual responsibility is still power-

[2] See in this connection David Riesman, *Individualism Reconsidered,* Free Press, 1954.

ful—a statement so obvious that one would apologize for making it were it not for a persistent tendency to view the law as social pattern rather than ethical drama. Yet the spectator, as he looks upon the prisoner at the bar in any important trial, must say to himself, "There but for the grace of God go I"; and anyone cognizant of what is discussed when a jury deliberates must know that the allocation of responsibility usually determines the decision. American sports are commonly cited as examples of teamwork and therefore of social adjustment, but the winning pitcher in a world series, the winning jockey in a Kentucky Derby, the current lightweight champion of the world are in their several spheres as gravely studied as are the individual characters we know as statesmen or literary geniuses. "Leadership," too, is a favorite American word; and though few Americans realize how closely this national doctrine skirts the *Führerprinzip* that ruined Germany, the president, the secretary of state, the secretary of agriculture, the senator, the governor, the mayor are still thought of as outstanding persons capable of making decisions and accepting responsibility for them.

But perhaps the most interesting development in the contemporary doctrine of individualism is found in industry itself. Capital and labor have both discovered that *expertise* is not enough, that, as somebody has said, animals specialize and can do nothing else, but man can take broader views. Labor sends its representatives back to the universities on labor fellowships for self-development and does not require that they shall study labor alone but opens the whole spectrum of knowledge, including the humanities, to them. Through patterns of worker education labor also enriches the lives of workingmen and of their families by acquainting them with great books, great art, great music, and great issues in philosophy. The aim is not better robots, the aim is better-rounded individuals.

Business proclaims that it wants the young man with a liberal education, not the mere accountant or economic specialist, and each year sends its junior executives back to college in order to develop them as human beings, not as vice-presidents. The program of the American Telephone and Telegraph Company at the University of Pennsylvania and other institutions is representative of others. The young executives sent there on company time are expected to study anything except the telephone business, everything except the specialty that brings them their monthly checks. Apparently the college of commerce, though it gives excellent training, does not furnish education; vocationalism proves to be something less than maturity, and, whether the motive be selfish or a combination of idealism and practicality, big business discovers at long last that philosophy *is* a guide to life. The striking fact in almost all these programs is that a leading role in adult education is almost invariably given to the humanities. They, it is felt, strengthen and enrich the individual.

3

But how? Why should the study of literature, a course in the history of art, an analysis of Beethoven's symphonies, a discussion of Plato or William James strengthen and mature the individual? The American public is surrounded by the arts, yet complaint is made that individualism is weak. Why then will exposure to the humanistic treatment of literature, painting, music, and philosophy accomplish something that cheap books (available even in bootblacking establishments), popular magazines, "hit" music on the radio, television shows, the movies, reproductions of pretty pictures, and clearly written articles in *Time* and the *Reader's Digest* have failed to accomplish? What magic is there in the humanities?

Let us distinguish art from entertainment. Most popular fiction, most magazines, the instruments of mass communication like the radio and television, most movies, many pictures ranging from bank calendars to copies of "September Morn" are products of something called the entertainment industry. The entertainment industry seeks to make money by pleasing as many people as it can and by offending as few persons as it can. The entertainers it hires are conscientious, hard-working craftsmen. They earn their money, and they earn it honestly by pleasing a multitude of customers. Clearly, entertainment has an important place in American culture. Moreover, our instruments of mass communication have brought more fun into existence and banished more boredom than was ever possible before in history. The assertion that if Shakespeare were alive he would be writing for Hollywood makes a good deal of sense, even if it does not make whole sense. The example of George Gershwin shows, indeed, how a man of great talent can lift a popular form like jazz into a rather high form of symphonic music. One can complain that one issue of a popular magazine is very like another issue of the same magazine, and yet agree with Elmer Davis in believing that the clever men who edit these magazines give the public a better grade of fiction than it wholly deserves. One can even admire the drawing in certain comic strips without letting culture down. In sum, the popular arts are not to be condemned because they are popular. Only, they must not be mistaken for art. They are entertainment, and they seek to entertain.

Inevitably, therefore, most magazines, most television and radio shows, most movies, most of the "features" in the newspaper, most inspirational speakers do not get paid to excite differences of thought, but to soothe an audience. Mass media do not exist to manufacture points of view; they manufacture thrills. The staple of most short stories and most novels is either physical adventure or romantic love or both, but romantic love, physical adventure, thrills, and a sense of being soothed cannot of themselves carry the weight of living. The synonyms of *entertainment* are words like *amusement, diversion, sport, play, relaxation,* and *recreation,* and, by definition, to be relaxed, or sportive, or amused, or diverted is to be turned away from the central to the marginal aspect of life. One may reasonably complain if philosophy, however disguised, is thrust down one's throat when one is seeking relaxation, but not all the relaxation in the world will shape a philosophic character. Americans have a phrase for anybody who devotes his life to entertainment—they call him a *playboy.* Entertainers are not playboys, but those whom they entertain frequently fail to develop out of the playboy stage.

In *The Voices of Silence,* a fascinating book on the history of art in which the author tries to move art out of the cold-storage atmosphere of museums into the sunlit quality of the human—and humane—activity it truly is, André Malraux, opening a discussion of the creative process, distinguishes between the way an artist looks at the world and at art and the way a non-artist sees them. Much that he says is relevant to the important distinction between art and entertainment. The non-artist, Malraux points out, is not so much indifferent to the arts as convinced that they are merely means of expressing emotions. Every popular art—that is, every art appropriate to a mass medium—expresses sentimental yearning, sadness, gaiety, patriotism, love, or a vague idealism. Thus the man who has no real taste for music loves sentimental songs and military marches, the man who is bored by poetry likes magazine stories,[3] the man who does not care for painting likes

[3] Or carries in his wallet a favorite piece by James Whitcomb Riley or Eugene Field, which he reads to friends.

photographs of movie starlets or cats in baskets. Those who do not understand art vaguely regard it only as a way of recording emotional moments or of conjuring them up imaginatively. They confuse representation with painting, just as they think the only business of a novelist is to "tell a story." (One might as well argue that the only business of Shakespeare in *Hamlet* is to kill a king!) The man in the street believes that the painter's eye is just like his, only somehow mysteriously keener; and a painter is therefore somebody trained to single out an exceptional scene or person and record what he sees with photographic exactness.

But, as M. Malraux points out, the painter is not "inspired" by a scene but by the tradition of art, that is, by other paintings and the way they were made; and his vision is not the vision of the man in the street. The man in the street, when he looks at anything, looks at it in a way that is at once synthetic and incoherent. He sees, or thinks he sees, everything, but he cannot tell you what it is he sees. His vision wanders when its object is widespread (an "unframed" vision, say, of the Grand Canyon) and becomes tense, yet imprecise, when its object is a striking scene (the opposite wall of the Grand Canyon, with its suggestion of fearful depth). It achieves focus only when it is directed toward some act; as, for example, when, in looking at a wide landscape, somebody says, "Oh, see that man chopping wood over there!" But the painter is not interested in the man chopping wood; if he is interested in him at all, it will be only as a concentration point of color in a possible picture. The painter's vision, like that of the man in the street, achieves focus through an act, but the act is the act of painting. The painter's eye is conditioned by his previous experience with paintings by other painters and his previous experience with his own canvases. His professional business is to change the function of objects; *i.e.,* the woodcutter is not for him a man cutting wood, but a detail to be ignored or built up in terms of light and shade or color.

The point becomes clearer if one considers the problem of making a portrait. The eyes of the sitter are an essential component of a good portrait and of the "expression" the painter gives the face. But most of us never look at an eye as a thing in itself. Most of us do not know the color of the iris in the eyes of even our closest friends. For us the eye is essentially "a look." Only the oculist and the painter see the eye as a thing in itself. In short, the painter's whole way of seeing, when he is professionally engaged, differs wholly from that of the ordinary person. It is conditioned by his profession, and this has little or nothing to do with amusement. Says M. Malraux:

Artists do not stem from their childhood, but from their conflict with the achievements of their predecessors; not from their own formless world, but from their struggle with the forms which others have imposed on life. . . . Whenever we have records enabling us to trace the origins of a painter's, a sculptor's, any artist's vocation, we trace it not to a sudden vision or uprush of emotion (suddenly given form), but to the vision, the passionate emotion, or the serenity of another artist.[4]

Postponing for a moment longer the relation of the humanities to individual growth, let us revert to the amusement arts. They serve, as we have said, the socially useful function of relaxation. But relaxation is both literally and figuratively the opposite of bracing, and the amusement arts cannot long brace anybody for the battle of life. Theirs is a perpetually sunlit, a perpetually moonlit universe. In

---

[4] André Malraux, *The Voices of Silence,* trans. by Stuart Gilbert, Doubleday, 1953, p. 281. But see the whole illuminating discussion in the beginning of Part III, "The Creative Process," from which our text draws heavily.

their world love is forever "romantic," sorrow fleets, childhood is innocently mischievous, all males are either virtuous or "mean," all women are virginal, or sirens, or sweet
little housewives and mothers (or grandmas), and old age
knows neither aches nor querulousness nor senility. The
detective triumphs in the cause of righteousness, the unjust politician forever fails, the villain is exposed, the tune
comes out right, the landscape is pretty, the world does
not know death (except for the wicked). This universe is
a universe without business worries, without irreparable
loss, without frustration, without lingering disease, without lasting injustice, without tragic disaster. It is, moreover, a world of perpetual social contacts, in which no one
is ever long alone, and, most important of all, it is a world
in which decisions are never really made. If the hero errs,
his error is not fatal, merely reversible; if the heroine errs,
she will be forgiven.

But when we pass from the world of art as amusement to
the greater world of humane art, how things deepen and
alter! How our notions of man's fate enrich themselves,
and how our concept of the individual grows in stature
and philosophy! *There,* Hamlet struggles with problems
like our own—whom shall he trust among his fellow men?
There, in Beethoven's *Eroica* the spirit exalts great leadership to the very skies only (for modern hearers) to lament
the fall of the hero when the idol is shattered. *There,* in
Rembrandt's painting of an old woman paring her nails,
not only the pathos of old age but the very enigma of life
haunt us perpetually. *There,* in Rodin's statue of St. John
the Baptist we behold incarnate the forever going forward
of humanity. *There,* in the figure of the blinded Oedipus
at Colonnos we find acquiescence, serenity, illumination.
But we cannot comprehend these and like creations casually, in a relaxed mood, as if Oedipus were a Greek detective story badly told, the *Eroica* existed, like "Smoke

Gets in Your Eyes," for its tuneful nostalgia, or Rembrandt's old woman were only a faded daguerreotype of Grandma on your dear father's side. Shakespeare, Beethoven, Rodin, Sophocles, and the rest are among the greatest minds and spirits humanity has ever seen, and we cannot comprehend them unless we wrestle with them as Jacob did with the angel, unless we grow somewhere nearer their stature and catch their vision of the heights and depths, the abysses and the tendernesses of life. "What other significance can our existence have," asks John MacMurray, "than to be ourselves fully and completely?" Shakespeare and Sophocles were themselves fully and completely; what can we do to grow into dimensions approximating theirs?

"Everyone who takes himself and life seriously," writes Dr. Karen Horney, "wants to be alone at times. Our civilization has so engulfed us in the externals of living that we have little understanding of this need, but its possibilities for personal fulfillment have been stressed by philosophies and religions of all times." [5] This is, so to speak, only a contemporary restatement of a much-quoted observation by Thoreau to the effect that most men live lives of quiet desperation—Thoreau, whose *Walden,* that revelation of the spiritual strength possible to solitude, continues to fascinate our overly organized society. But Thoreau's comment is, in turn, essentially only an upside-down comment on the belief of the founding fathers that the heart of civilization is that every human being is of right entitled to life, liberty, and the pursuit of happiness. The pursuit of happiness, by the by, is not the same thing as the pursuit of welfare nor the pursuit of a high standard of living. [6] These ideas, basic to the American notion of a good life for the individual, are not scientific terms and cannot be

[5] Karen Horney, *Our Inner Conflicts,* Norton, 1945, p. 73. The quotation from MacMurray is found on p. 183 of her book.

[6] Joseph Wood Krutch, "Are the Humanities Worth Saving?" *The Saturday Review,* June 11, 1955, p. 22.

defined in the language of social science. They are private matter, to which science as science and the social sciences with their emphasis upon group and mass contribute only indirectly and from a distance. The only durable meaning of "life" in this context is one's inner life, the only use of "liberty" is long-run freedom to enrich that inner life, and the only possible meaning of happiness lies in some less transient satisfaction than eating and drinking, getting and spending and being amused.

The reason so many men live lives of quiet desperation is commonly that they lack courage to acquire the kind of knowledge, the kind of value that will order their inward life otherwise. Their desperation comes from social pressure to keep up with the Joneses. Great individuals— Socrates, Lincoln, Jane Addams, Einstein, Michelangelo, Florence Nightingale, Spinoza—have never worried about keeping up with the Joneses. They have, instead, offered the Joneses an opportunity to climb a little nearer to *them,* on a plane of satisfaction beyond competition in material things. The record of these individuals—the meaning of the work they did, the lives they led—is principally (though of course not wholly) the possession of the humanities, and takes shape as art, philosophic thought, and example.

But mature understanding of art and philosophic thought is possible only by following their example of individual study, individual maturation. Man, even American man, will have to toil at the problem of comprehending the way a great painter, a great musician, a great poet, or a great philosopher sees life, just as he has to toil at understanding Keynesian economics, the business cycle, or the physics and chemistry of refining oil. The difference is that the arts and philosophy interpret life, and that, studying these interpretations, the individual matures as an individual, not merely as a business executive or a technician. He becomes aware of heights and depths of emotion and thought, of ranges of experience and satisfaction his business or his vocation cannot give him.

The sympathetic, the mature understanding of this simple, yet difficult truth is something logic cannot give. In all probability it must be taken as a matter of faith, almost as if it were a matter of religion. It cannot be taught through group pressures, pedagogical devices, or subliminal feed-back systems. It cannot be acquired in the arts of entertainment. It is true that the untrained auditor gets something out of great music, if it is no more than the "tune" in the first movement of Schubert's *Unfinished Symphony;* the untrained viewer gets an impression of color from Turner's "Rain, Speed, Steam," though he doesn't know what the picture is all about and wonders why it isn't clearer; the untrained reader can follow the story of *Romeo and Juliet;* and the untrained thinker can turn William James's theory that the test of a truth lies in its practical effects into the doctrine that whatever practically succeeds must be "true." But all this leaves music, painting, and literature at the entertainment level, and sentimentalizes philosophy. Schubert becomes "My Song of Love," Turner's colors turn up in a three-color press-work advertisement for firearms, *Romeo and Juliet* is burlesqued, and pragmatism transmogrified into a volume of "inspirational thinking." The auditor, the viewer, the reader, the "thinker" in these instances experience no individual development, but only confirmation. Nothing challenges the ear, the eye, or the mind. Yet the universal experience of mankind has been that the individual can no more develop without challenge to the mind, the heart, and the soul than he can improve his swimming by sitting in an armchair and dreaming about next summer's vacation.

4

The distinction between the august demands of art and thought and the more fleeting satisfactions honestly offered by the entertainment industry is fundamental, but the difference must not be misconstrued into an attack on the popular arts by the high-brow. It is as wrongheaded for the humanist to scorn the popular arts as it is for the ignorant to scorn the humanities. The important truth, which American education has not yet quite learned, is not to mistake the function of the one for the function of the other, not to expect from the relaxation sold by the entertainment industry the intellectual challenge of the fine arts and of philosophy. Contrariwise, those who approach greatness in art, and profundity in philosophical, ethical, and religious discussions err if they assume that such art shall be instantly amusing and the statement of truths immediately evident. Great art like advanced science has no obligation to entertain. Its duty lies in the direction of illumination, depth, and growth. Illumination can be a gripping experience, but it is something quite different from entertainment. Both are necessary in our society.

One should also guard one's self from another possible misinterpretation. The fact that great art and profound thought are difficult to comprehend does not mean that simplified instruction in the humanities cannot be offered to beginners. On the contrary, wise introduction becomes the more necessary, just as is true in science. High-school pupils get something out of *Julius Caesar,* a reproduction in the classroom of Millet's "The Gleaners," a recording of "The Ride of the Valkyries," and Emerson's *The American Scholar.* But youth will never get beyond this "something" if these masterpieces are "taught" as if they did not differ from the latest Broadway comedy or television hit, the pictures in *Look,* a jazz record, and an inspirational message by some popular preacher. Introductory matter that never gets beyond introductions seldom leads to acquaintanceship. Complaint is made about science teaching in the secondary schools that textbooks have been so debased by the supposed demands of teaching that they are both obsolescent and unattractive; and it is to remedy this situation that, under a grant from the National Science Foundation, the Physical Science Study Committee is preparing textbooks in physics that will really introduce the beginning student to modern science and lead him to further study.[7] Many beginning books in literature, the arts, the languages, and, in some ways, ethics and philosophy are like the physics books complained of. They lead nowhere. They assume that what is contemporary or novel must alone be true and lasting. Their emphasis is upon entertainment and pleasure rather than upon challenge and instruction. If we really seek in our public education to mature American youth, we shall make small progress in the humanities unless our elementary work leads into greatness and not into the merely contemporary. The contemporary fades every year; the problems of humanity continue.

It has been remarked in the opening chapter that the enduring puzzles of life are not of a public and social nature, but are private and individual, like falling in love, the experience of disaster, or the glory of success. The personal experience of these profound events cannot be quantified. The anthropologists assure us that one exults or sorrows or endures according to one's value system, but most of us do not truly think so. We behave in these moments as our philosophy, conscious, half-conscious, or unconscious, teaches us to do, and our philosophy is, we

[7] See, as an example, *Physics,* Volume I, Preliminary Edition, Harvard University Press, 1957.

feel, the fusion of our experiences of life, of art, of emotion, and of whatever wisdom we may have gleaned from
the records of man. The revelations of life, art, emotion,
and wisdom gleaned from the records of man are, of
course, precisely what the humanities have to give. Theirs
is the area where, once we have mastered the language and
understood the technique of artist, writer, or philosopher,
we slowly learn ways of facing the unpredictable and
reconciling ourselves to what is inevitable. By so doing we
transform ourselves and, in the long run, transform society.

But here again let us be clear. Few of us, when a beloved
parent dies, take to reading *Paradise Lost,* though many
may turn to the Bible. To suppose that the humanities
have a specific to offer in every such case is to assume that
art and philosophy can be turned into pills for particular
persons. Individual maturation is as gradual in matters of
spiritual and philosophical value as is individual maturation in business, science, and the conduct of public affairs.
The wisdom of some of the training programs for labor
leaders and business executives already mentioned lies precisely in this: that they commonly take at least a year, they
are not "short courses" or "retread" programs. You cannot
make up a list of five books that will automatically reduce
sorrow. You cannot put together a list of piano compositions that will with the accuracy of medicine lessen loneliness. You cannot even say what philosopher or religious
outlook—Buddha, Plato, Jesus, Aquinas, Spinoza, Schopenhauer, Emerson—is "right" for a particular person.
But you can, if you go about it with patience and humility, acquire from the humanities a point of view, an angle
of vision concerning yourself and the world that will
simultaneously assist you in developing both unity and detachment—an inward unity that will make for personal
integrity, a detachment from too great an engagement
with the immediate that does in the long run protect in-

tegrity. But you cannot accomplish this by expecting the humanities to operate on you as entertainment or by approaching art, philosophy, and religion as if they were at fault in not producing results in six weeks.

"Each discipline," writes the Canadian humanist F. E. L. Priestley, "seeks its own kind of pattern, and has its own criteria of validity." We grant this without reservation in the case of science, or economics, or psychology, but in the case of the humanities we persistently confuse the issue. The next portion of Mr. Priestley's paragraph suggests the cause of our confusion. He writes:

A good poem is as true as a scientific law; if it is read by generations of readers who recognize in it a real correspondence to their own experience, and particularly if it illuminates for readers the quality of their own experience, they rightly call the poem "true to life." Those of us trained in the humanities take all this for granted; we know why Arnold calls poetry "a criticism of life"; but those who, in Browning's phrase, think of poetry as "a substitute for a good cigar" would seek elsewhere, in psychologists' casebooks, in sociologists' statistics, for the "hard facts." For his part, the student of literature would be perhaps too ready to assert that the reality which psychologist and sociologist sought unsuccessfully was already fully presented in literature. This . . . constitutes the real problem; there is a failure of understanding of aims and methods, and a reluctance to grant validity as truth to the products of other studies.[8]

This is a wise warning to humanists, but, taken in reverse, as it were, it is also wise counsel to those who seek maturity through the humanities.

For great art, when it is "true to life," is not true to life in any photographic sense. The work of art does not operate in a one-to-one relationship between the reader (or

---

[8] "Problems of a Three-Dimensional Education," *Transactions of the Royal Society of Canada*, XLVIII, 3d series, June, 1954, Section 2, p. 43.

auditor or spectator) and itself; and to expect such a relationship is to miss the whole power of art. You do not have to commit murder to be moved by *Crime and Punishment, Othello* throws virtually no light upon the problem of desegregating schools in the United States, and the erotic longing of *Tristan und Isolde* does not drive the audience out to commit a thousand adulteries. Contrariwise, I cannot expect an artist or a philosopher literally to anticipate, parallel, and share my private life. The problem is at once simpler and more complicated. It is simpler in the sense that if I will but yield to the artist or the philosopher—and yielding in this context means the necessity of understanding his technical problem, his point of view, and, however vaguely, the intellectual climate of the time in which he lived—he can point out to me the long-run significance of great primary issues of import to many thousands of thoughtful human beings. It is more complicated because—well, because every man is as lazy as he dares to be, and "learning" is a difficult concept. Learning lacks the vocational drive. It changes nothing immediately. Its profits lie dimly in the future. But there is a saying attributed to Confucius that ought to give us pause: "Study without thought is vain, and thought without study is dangerous."

FOUR

The Humanities
and the National Culture

Let us go back again to our businessman and his questions. Among other things, he wanted to know what he could do about the humanities in relation to the community and its life. Let us now ask what the relation between the humanities and the national culture is.

Americans are aware of something in their life called culture, and many of them know that the humanities have something to do with it. It is, however, also a part of the American tradition to say that culture is of no special concern to the average man, but is something for high-brows, or for leisure hours, or for persons like ministers, teachers, educators, artists, and (if one may dare say so) women's clubs. If the average citizen feels any responsibility for culture, it is sporadic responsibility, like his sporadic interest in the parent-teacher association. Let us ask, therefore, whether the immense importance of the humanities to our general life cannot be more adequately defined. By way of beginning let us repeat the list of the branches of humane learning: philosophy in all its parts, the languages, literature, the fine arts and music, the decorative arts, the arts of the theater, folklore, archaeology, history, and many aspects of anthropology, economics, and other social sciences not to be severed from their humanistic implications.

You cannot, for example, understand the Declaration of Independence or the Constitution of the United States, both documents in political science, without some acquaintance with eighteenth-century philosophy, and you cannot altogether comprehend modern economics without some grasp upon its historical development since Adam Smith published *The Wealth of Nations* in 1776.

An excellent rule-of-thumb method to ascertain the importance of any component of a problem is to see what would happen if in imagination you could permanently remove the component from the problem. If, for example, all knowledge of science were to vanish overnight from the United States, industry, the national defense, agriculture, medicine, public health, engineering, transportation, and much else would be so instantly crippled, we would cease to be a great power and would fall back into some form of primitive agrarian, pastoral, or perhaps merely tribal society. If all knowledge of modern economics were blotted out, our business system, our governments, our national life would collapse, and we would revert of necessity to a barter system and have painfully to relearn from that point what we had lost. What would happen if the humanities were permanently to disappear?

It is by now evident, one hopes, that the humanities include our knowledge of the past. Contemporary art and thought are sometimes assumed to have no relation to the past because they rebel against it. But contemporary thought and art are contemporary only because of tradition. The most radical thinker, the unpredictable work of art, the latest novelty in music, the theater, the dance, or anything else is radical, or unpredictable, or novel only as knowledge of the past makes it so. Brought up in some sort of tradition, the artist or the thinker has rebelled violently against it. But he cannot rebel unless the tradition exists, nor can we know he is rebelling against anything unless we know what it is he rebels against.[1] In imagining the humanities to disappear permanently from American life we are therefore forced to remove, along with all works of art, all scholarship about the humanities, and all that we may call humane learning. If the humanities disappear, humane learning disappears with them; and if humane learning disappears, the humanities also go. Although this has probably never happened in the history of the West, a state like ancient Sparta came close to this curious condition.

What would vanish? All formal knowledge of language and all formal knowledge of languages, ancient and modern, would be gone. There could be no grammars, dictionaries, or textbooks. The capacity to translate anything from one language into another, except viva voce, would die out, since the tradition of formal literary expression would vanish. We could not interpret the Bible, since we would have no orderly acquaintance with Hebrew, Greek, and Latin. Because we would have no orderly acquaintance with any other language, we would be equally baffled as to the meaning of any classic—Homer, Shakespeare, Proust. The unifying force of the public schools in language would weaken and die in the absence of proper textbooks and be replaced perhaps by oral traditions that would vary more and more from region to region and eventually become unintelligible to each other. Publishing would be severely handicapped and might disappear. Communication between man and man would grow more and more *ad hoc*.

Since all philosophy would likewise go except such as we could naïvely invent on the spur of the moment, it would be difficult and probably impossible to enunciate

---

[1] The most extreme form of modern rebellion in the arts has possibly been the Dadaist movement of the twenties, which denied that there is anything like a tradition of beauty or a tradition of reason. But ideas of beauty and reason had to exist before they could be denied.

any general principle whether in science, or in mathematics, or in ethics, or in law. Because we would then have no acquaintance with the laborious steps by which thinkers like Plato and Kant arrived at significant meanings for words such as God, cause, justice, perfection, and so on, our lawmaking ability would be mortally injured. We, or our descendants, would by and by stare at language like the following without comprehending it, as Turkish shepherds stared uncomprehendingly at inscriptions on Roman arches in Asia Minor:

We the People of the United States, in Order to form a more perfect Union, establish Justice, insure domestic Tranquility, provide for the common defence, promote the general Welfare, and secure the Blessings of Liberty to ourselves and our Posterity . . .

It is likewise possible that all religious concepts except rudimentary ones like fear and propitiation would dwindle and die.

For a time the conduct of literature would be unaffected, but by and by the meaning of such forms as the novel, the short story, the ode, the epic, and so on would become merely traditional and would in the long run disappear, since there would be no knowledge of the past of art, and writing, if it survived, might again be reduced to simple anecdotal narrative. Quarrels over the styles of public buildings, domestic architecture (for example, a Frank Lloyd Wright house), churches, business blocks, and so on would die out, for all historical knowledge of styles would go. Paintings would become more and more meaningless for lack of information about them, as the ruins of Roman buildings became meaningless in the early Middle Ages, when peasants and their betters used the Colosseum for a quarry. Public monuments as such would vanish—the Lincoln Memorial would, in time, be neglected, since nobody would know who Lincoln was, or it might be either destroyed as a monument to an evil spirit or cherished as the temple of a god. There would by and by be only vacant lots where libraries and museums once stood; inasmuch as we have imagined all knowledge of the humanities to disappear, the principal deposits of humanistic lore would have to disappear also.

The basis of behavioral science would also be altered. Probably such elementary matters as the family, parental love, the in-group and the out-group would not be much affected by the change, but anthropologists would have some difficulty in finding anything to measure from or measure by, in their estimates of community behavior, and of course such concepts as an Oedipus complex would have to be renamed or reworked by psychiatrists and others. We would have no knowledge of either linguistics or archaeology. Surveyors of public opinion would face unexpected difficulties: what kinds of "public" opinion on what sorts of subjects would they survey? For example, anti-Semitism is based on the supposed history of the Jews, but there would be no cultural history, right or wrong, in this queer world. We could not understand Marxism, since nobody would know anything about Marx; we could not understand "Hispanism," since nobody would know anything about Hispanic culture and its history; and, for that matter and to us most important of all, we could not understand "Americanism," since the statement that all men are created equal and are endowed by their Creator with certain unalienable rights would be unintelligible.

2

The great cultures of history have been notable not for the absence of humane learning but for its vital presence. There is, of course, no way of measuring human happi-

ness, especially the happiness of men long dead, and there
is some truth in the adage: Happy is that people whose
annals are short. Nevertheless, throughout recorded time
wise men have regarded those cultures as memorable
which have fostered learning. We remember the genius of
Athens, not the Spartan army. The legacy of Rome, we
think, is a legacy of law, not of legions, valuable as the
legions were in maintaining law. Egypt is for us more than
a repetitious tale of conquest and retreat across the Sinai
Peninsula; it is the majesty of pyramid and temple and
statue, the enigma of the Sphinx. Attila, that redoubtable
Scourge of God, counts for nothing beside the unwarlike
Goethe, whose only military experience was to gaze from
afar on the bloodless Battle of Valmy. We owe more to
Florence and Weimar than we do to Gibraltar and Port
Arthur, more to little Judaea than to great Babylon, more
to Buddha than to Tamerlane and Genghis Khan. The
perdurable contributions of a culture are not material
power, military might, sensual indulgence, or business
success; the lasting value of civilizations is not a function
of their geographic spread nor of the terrors they inspired
in their neighbors, but lies in the ideas they nourished,
in the men of art, science, and learning who incarnated
these ideas. This is the kind of greatness the founders of
the United States dreamed of. In their dream, learning was
a central fact.

Learning, in truth, reached America earlier than did the
social sciences and quite as early as science.[2] The number
of cultivated men who came to seventeenth-century Virginia was phenomenal, as were the number of college grad-

[2] Even a casual reading in Hakluyt's *Voyages,* that great collection of
travels (*The Principal Navigations, Voyages, Traffics and Discoveries of the
English Nation,* 3 vols., 1598–1600; now available in Everyman's Library),
shows how eagerly the men of the Renaissance in sailing to the New World
sought to increase geographical, astronomical, botanical, zoological, and
anthropological information.

uates who came to seventeenth-century New England. The charter of the oldest American university establishes Harvard College "to advance Learning and perpetuate it to Posterity," and similar aims created William and Mary, Yale, Columbia (King's College), Princeton (the College of New Jersey), and the rest. State constitutions adopted immediately after 1776 often include the creation of a state university among their provisions, so that, on paper at least, popular faith in learning was first expressed by the University of Georgia and the University of North Carolina as tax-supported schools. The Ordinance of 1787 for the governing of the Northwest Territory proclaimed an axiomatic relation between freedom and learning and declared that the means of education must be forever encouraged. The founding of the American Philosophical Society at Philadelphia in 1749, of the American Academy of Arts and Sciences in Boston in 1780, and of the American Antiquarian Society in Worcester in 1812 is further evidence. The men who signed the Declaration and who drafted the Constitution were, as a group, whether they were businessmen, lawyers, landholders, physicians, or soldiers, characteristically humane in training and outlook.[3] In 1800 federal legislation created the Library of

[3] It is interesting to read the "loose sketches and notes" of Major William Pierce, a delegate from Georgia to the Constitutional Convention. He writes of Washington: "Like Gustavus Vasa, he may be said to be the deliverer of his Country;—like Peter the great he appears as the politician and the Statesman; and like Cincinnatus he returned to his farm perfectly contented with being only a plain Citizen, after enjoying the highest honor of the Confederacy,—and now only seeks for the approbation of his Countrymen by being virtuous and useful." He describes a less prominent member in these terms: "Mr. Ingersol [Jared Ingersoll of Pennsylvania] is a very able Attorney, and possesses a clear legal understanding. He is well educated in the Classics, and is a Man of very extensive reading. Mr. Ingersol speaks well, and comprehends his subject fully. There is a modesty in his character that keeps him back. He is about 36 years old." Small wonder that enthusiastic British liberals characterized the men of the convention as a congregation of demigods! See *Documents Illustrative of the Formation of the Union of the American States,* Washington, Government Printing Office, 1927, pp. 96–108.

Congress, now one of the great book collections of the world. Colonial and revolutionary merchants showed by their gifts to colleges a profound belief in learning, and pioneered the way for later benevolence, the theory of which was expressed by Andrew Carnegie's famous "The Gospel of Wealth" (1900), which teaches that riches are not a private possession but create a social duty to the culture of the nation. Stephen Girard in one half-century, Ezra Cornell in another, founded institutions of learning, and their examples have been paralleled at The Johns Hopkins University, Stanford, the University of Chicago, Case Institute, Duke, Tulane, Rice, and many others. Business wealth maintains the Folger Library, the Huntington Library and Art Museum, the Frick Gallery, the Boston Museum, the Clements Library and so on; and without business wealth the Metropolitan Opera, and great symphony orchestras from Boston to San Francisco would die overnight. Americans have done this because, in the words of Carl L. Becker, they believed that "the best case for democracy, and the best reason for having faith in the freedom of learning and teaching which it fosters, is that in the long history of civilization humanity has proved stronger than hate, and falsehood less enduring than truth." [4]

In America, then, learning has not characteristically lacked support, nor has our dependence upon learning as an essential component of culture ever ceased, though it has sometimes been obscured. Today the great foundations are interested in the humanities. Government is concerned to make available the treasures of the past through libraries, museums, and schools. Labor wants to enrich the lives of workers through adult education,[5] and groups of

[4] *Freedom and Responsibility in the American Way of Life*, Knopf, 1945, p. 64.

[5] On the estate of a former millionaire (Bayberry Land, on Long Island, near Southampton) thirty members of Local 3 of the International Brother-

all kinds hear speakers and discuss problems in art, philosophy, literature, ethics, and general values. Nor are the
churches silent.

Yet, despite this eagerness, the battle to sustain humane
learning at proper levels has not been easy, and is not easy
today. In one phase of our history "practical" demands
momentarily overwhelm humane learning; in other periods brilliant technological achievement seems to assure
effortless happiness in perpetuity. Why, then, bother with
the past, or with the arts, or with thinking? Eras of armed
conflict also momentarily diminish interest in the humanities and increase the immediate appeal of other disciplines.
Thus, one effect of the Civil War was to increase the
number of engineering schools, military needs during
World War I created the National Research Council, and
out of World War II emerged the Atomic Energy Commission. A cultural imbalance may be then created. Such
a situation seems to exist today.

3

What is the nature of this cultural imbalance? The student
of American opinion learns to expect stock responses to
this question. One such is the charge of materialism; that
is, Americans are supposed to be intent upon wealth in
contrast to Europeans, who are intent on culture, but the
charge is meaningless. The love of money is a universal

hood of Electrical Workers come each week without charge and with
their wages paid for that week to study the elements of such disciplines
as logic, semantics, economics, and history. "The sole aim of the venture
is, through increased thinking ability, to make them happier, more useful
citizens at home, on the job, and in the community." The course of study
was suggested by Dean Harry Carman of Columbia College, and between
June, 1956, and October, 1957, about 455 men had passed through the
course, half of whom had never got past grade school. See the article by
A. H. Raskin in the New York *Times* for November 3, 1957. Other unions
have analogous programs.

passion, as the American tourist haggling over prices in Istanbul, Paris, or Panama soon learns. Equally meaningless are other stock allegations such as vulgarity, violence, noisiness, superficiality, bad manners, sentimentality, bad taste, softness, bad grammar, and the like. It would be invidious to rank cultures by their defects, and these failings are universal among nations. Some Europeans and some Asians of course deny the existence of American culture, but a country that has produced Willard Gibbs, Thomas Jefferson, Walt Whitman, Frank Lloyd Wright, George Gray Barnard, Jane Addams, William James, Abraham Lincoln, Benjamin Franklin, George Gershwin, and others, not to speak of the Boston Symphony Orchestra, the Institute for Advanced Study, the National Gallery, the paintings of Thomas Eakins and Albert Pinkham Ryder, Golden Gate Park, the Brooklyn Bridge, Rockefeller Center, and the Skyline Drive through the Great Smokies is no more to be judged by its jukeboxes than is France by the Folies-Bergère, Great Britain by bank-holiday trippers, or Germany by its noisy motorcycles. The problem lies deeper.

Difficult though it be to analyze this complex situation, one can say that modern American culture falls into imbalance from the following three causes.

1. A mistaken attitude toward *knowledge.* Contemporary belief in the superiority of *expertise,* whether it be embodied in the radio repairman or in those charged with launching an artificial satellite, overshadows the concept of general knowledge. Moreover, a misunderstanding of science leads many to think that "scientific method" can be applied to almost any department of life. When, for example, a "scientific" study of ethics proves that all moral judgments are relative, it is next inferred that *all* value judgments must therefore be relative also. Truth comes to be thought of as something quantitative or statistical,

something arrived at through the calculus, or tabulation, or, better still, through a digital computer; all other truth, emotional, aesthetic, imaginative, religious, which in a general sense may be called traditional, turns into something more or less untrustworthy, though it may give pleasure in one's idle hours. Hence it follows—and the decline in the workday gives the doctrine special fascination—that books, music, the arts, most philosophy, and most religious ideas are, in the words of school superintendents, "worthy leisure-time activities," but not an essential part of one's active life. Symbolic is the exaltation of the engineer and the technologist, and the decline in the prestige of the minister. Significant, also, is the relegation of philosophers, artists, writers, painters, and musicians to a marginal place in economic life. Thus, the unemployment of engineers becomes a problem, but the continual unemployment problem in the fine arts is merely regrettable.

2. A misunderstanding of the nature and limits of *social action*. Traditionally, America is the land of rugged individualism, although during the pioneer phase the necessity for communal activities[6] and the push toward conformity were evident. During the post-Civil War period, while spokesmen for business, industry, and public affairs continued to praise individualism (the so-called "Protestant Ethic"), the need to assimilate millions of immigrants, social pressures in our mushrooming cities, and the astonishing efflorescence of the social sciences combined with other forces to make social adjustment desirable. In the twentieth century psychological testing, personnel engineering, concepts of group organization, group research, group dynamics and the like, the theory that "co-operation carries its own ethic," and, negatively, fear of personal,

[6] Ranging from the husking bee and the house-raising to the defense of the stockade against marauders.

domestic, social, and emotional insecurity have further limited the area of individual action. [7] The McCarthy episode helped to substitute for stick-to-itiveness the cynical twentieth-century saw: "Don't stick your neck out." In education the fallacy takes shape in the assumption that engineers, or scientists, or businessmen, or teachers are "products" of "training" and that in times of stress like the post-Sputnik era education can be speeded up to "deliver" more and better scientists. Meantime, every commencement speaker greets the class as leaders of tomorrow, in periods of political tension angry editorials demand "leadership," and, always, enterprises as variegated as publishing, sports, science, industry, and interior decorating cry aloud for more "talent." Another ritualistic demand is for "men of imagination." But the incompatibility of simultaneously demanding originality and requiring conformity is clear, and the effect is to weaken decision-making. Since responsibility can be referred to a committee, an adviser, a cabinet, a staff, a sales conference, or an opinion analysis, why stick your neck out? If you are loyal, why also be original? There are, of course, vigorous individuals in American life, but our interest here is in cultural imbalance.[8]

[7] In *The Organization Man,* a skeptical but intelligent account of the social organization of American business, William H. Whyte, Jr., of *Fortune* contrasts traditional belief that "pursuit of individual salvation through hard work, thrift and competitive struggle is the heart of the American achievement" with the current creed of the junior executive: "Be loyal to the company and the company will be loyal to you. After all, if you do a good job for the organization, it is only good sense for the organization to be good to you, because that will be best for everybody. There are a bunch of real people around here. Tell them what you think and they will respect you for it. They don't want a man to fret and stew about his work. It won't happen to me. A man who gets ulcers probably shouldn't be in business anyway" (Simon & Schuster, 1956; Anchor Books, 1957, p. 142). Contrast: "John Marshall has made his decision—let him enforce it!"

[8] In his annual report for 1954–55 the dean of the Harvard Law School, declaring a graduate "should be prepared to be a wise and informed

3. Intertwined with these two characteristics but having other implications is a *mistrust of thought*. Anti-intellectualism is presumably a universal human failing, and practicality has long been a standard American trait. An important contemporary trend, however, creates a genuine lack of respect for the powers of the human mind, despite the awe generated by a name like Einstein. This trend is the product of several misunderstandings. One arises from undue stress upon *ad hoc* performance or technological skills. Americans have always admired that clever fellow the inventor, who, without knowing much basic science, applies science to life in ways those plodding men the theoretical scientists never dream of. Why, then, bother with the philosophy of the subject, when cunning machines seem to circumvent the necessity of thought, and demands from industry or government raise a thousand fascinating immediate questions of application? Moreover, in the age of relativity all theories are relative also, are mere tools to be used or cast aside, but not eternal ideas. A wide popular misconception of the significance of psychology in the post-Freudian world further diminishes respect for mind, since it is inferred that all motives are subrational, all conduct shaped by social pressures and

lawyer and leader in his community" no less than a person of general culture, lamented the trend in prelegal education. A sampling of the transcripts of applicants for admission showed that in an embarrassing number of cases the student had had no work at all in literature, philosophy, a foreign language, sociology, government, natural science, or mathematics, but presented instead courses in "Typography, Principles of Advertising, Reporting, Advertising Copy and Finance, Introduction to Advertising, Advertising Procedures, and Sales Management; or Office Management, Principles of Retailing, Salesmanship, and Principles of Marketing; or Scene Design, Stage Lighting, Producing, Advanced Acting, and Playwriting; or Organization and Administration of Playgrounds, Methods in Minor Sports, Theory of Play and Recreation, Camping and Playgrounds, and Coaching Baseball and Track." "If the law is to be a cultured profession," he concluded, "it might be as well to make it plainer that an exclusive diet of this sort of thing is not looked on with favor as far as this School is concerned" (p. 11). Note that the courses listed are either merely "training" or dominated by a philosophy of social action.

unconscious desires, all "reason" self-seeking "rationalization." Disturbed personalities, mental cases, the vogue of the psychoanalyst, the manipulation of public opinion through propaganda and advertising skillfully controlled by experts—elements like these are interpreted to mean that human reason is a mere shell over a dark, primitive psyche, a view confirmed by memories of the success of Nazi leaders in leading a whole nation astray. One disturbing result is the inability of Americans to present a coherent, sensible, and persuasive philosophy of democracy to the monolithic rationalism of communist theory, which is nothing if not "rational." Perhaps for that reason many Americans distrust rationalism all the more. This trend, is, of course, countered by an unshakable belief in the capacity of American education to develop a "well-rounded" personality and to mature the mind of the scholar even though he graduates into a world of unreason.

4

Such seem to be important aspects of our cultural imbalance. Humane learning is not a pill to be swallowed in order that the ailing may be instantly restored to health, nor is it for a moment assumed that only humanists possess cultural wisdom. Science, social science, and the humanities, rightly understood, are inseparable parts of human knowledge, elements showing mutual interdependence in the development of man. But our present concern *is* with the humanities and with the responsibility of humane learning for national culture. What is that responsibility?

The central value of the humanities to American culture has never been better phrased than by Judge Learned Hand speaking to the Regents of the University of the State of New York in 1952. I shall argue, he said, that the humanities, instead of being regarded only as a solace, a refuge, and an enrichment of the individual—as indeed they are—are also an essential factor in training him to perform his duties in a democratic society, as important even as acquaintance with the persons and the current events on which he is called to pass. There is, he said bluntly, no substitute for an open mind enriched by reading and the arts.

He could see no escape from a calculation of, a balance among, group interests in American society, each having its own desires and values. But desires and values are not quantitatively measurable, for they seldom have any common constituents, and without these they cannot be objectively compared.

It would be easy to choose between the desires and values of conflicting social groups, if we could safely impute to them our own preferences. But by what right can we do so; and, if we cannot, what other means of vicarious choice have we? I submit that we have none except in so far as we can imaginatively project ourselves into the position of the groups between which we must choose. . . . It is not enough to be personally detached, although that is of course a condition; we must also acquire a capacity for an informed sympathy with, and an understanding of, the desires and values of others; and that, I submit, only those who have any chance of attaining whose experience is supplemented by some acquaintance, the wider the better, with what others have thought and felt in circumstances as near as possible to those of the groups in question.

I dare hope, said the Judge, I have made it clear "why I am arguing that an education which includes the 'humanities' is essential to political wisdom."

By "humanities" I especially mean history; but close beside history and of almost, if not quite, equal importance are letters, poetry, philosophy, the plastic arts, and music. Most of the issues that mankind sets out to settle, it never does settle.

. . . [The issue] disappears because it is replaced by some compromise that . . . offers a tolerable substitute for victory; and he who would find the substitute needs an endowment as rich as possible in experience . . . an experience which makes the heart generous and provides his mind with an understanding of the hearts of others.

"I cannot but think," Judge Hand concluded, "that we of this generation are politically in especial need of such education." [9] It needs scarcely to be added that in a democracy the need for such an education in order to make these choices falls upon all of us, including scientists, businessmen, technologists, and scholars.

It is difficult or impossible to dispute so sagacious an observer. If the humanities have this responsible role in our society, they cannot live a kind of hole-and-counter existence, coming out, so to speak, only on Sundays.[10] Our colleges and universities cannot become branches of a great intellectual cartel manufacturing well-adjusted Americans, nor turn into factories producing technicians prepared to manipulate the devices by which the twentieth century goes about its own destruction. Most men and women in this republic are not scientists, nor are they going to be. Their lives are occupied with economic problems, religious problems, domestic problems, governmental problems that every day require individual sagacity.[11] Nor, while we are on this matter, should we misinterpret depth psychology to mean that all values are both relative and hypocritical; to do so is to be frightened to death by

[9] Learned Hand, "Freedom and the Humanities," *American Association of University Professors Bulletin*, 38, Winter 1952–53, pp. 520–527.

[10] "Until kids learn from their elders to respect the man who carries his wealth between his ears as much as the one who drives it around in a glitter of chrome, we're going to get into deeper and deeper trouble." Bill Mauldin, "Notes on KP and/or the Egghead," New York *Times Magazine*, December 8, 1957, p. 36.

[11] See George Boas, "The Humanities and the Sciences," *The Peabody Reflector*, October, 1956.

a ventriloquist. The attitude of sensible psychiatrists is expressed by Dr. Karen Horney when she writes: "My own belief is that man has the capacity as well as the desire to develop his own potentialities. . . . I believe that man can change and go on changing as long as he lives." [12] Nations are people, not automats. "My own controller," said a vice-president of the Ford Motor Company, "says to me with great wisdom: 'The technical problems we can lick—the really tough problems are people.' " [13] But even this shrewd statement must be amended: the controller is not confronted by people, which is an amorphous, a statistical concept; he is confronted by individuals who come before him in endless and varied procession, each living his own life, struggling with his own conscience, making his own decisions with intuitive, not scientific, wisdom, common sense, shortsightedness, folly, or criminality. This is the endless procession mirrored in art and interpreted by humane learning, and individual images in painting or music or poetry or drama remind us forever that we are men and women, not mass and crowd. Voters who demand leadership, industry which demands men of decision, the church, the Senate, the school crying out for richly endowed individuals are but echoing Emerson when he defined the scholar as man thinking. All our studies of decision making come back in the end to this: somebody has to decide, whether he live in the White House or anywhere else. But decisions are the products of imaginative projections into the points of view of other men and women; they are imaginative calculation of future event. They are good decisions only in proportion as they come from a decider whose life has been enhanced by an experi-

---

[12] *Our Inner Conflicts*, Norton, 1945, p. 19.
[13] Theodore O. Yntema, "A Liberal Education," *Address at Occidental College, Los Angeles, California,* May 10, 1957, p. 9.

ence of what the best and happiest minds can tell him.[14]

The art historian Bernard Berenson distinguishes true art from everything else by declaring it has a life-enhancing quality or value, and though part of his discussion is a little technical,[15] the heart of it lies precisely in the ideal of humane learning operative in modern society. The arts, literature, and philosophy, as somebody has said, constitute the noblest and happiest part of any nation's culture; the humanities are the most astonishing and exuberant of all the vehicles of human spirit, for they represent the creative zest and symbolic play which are undertaken for no purpose other than their good and natural selves. They sharpen our awareness of the full range of human thought and emotion; they instruct us by showing the possibilities of the human condition. If wise men are right in believing that the increase of consciousness is the index of human evolution, America will be known by its humanities, not by its average of social adjustment. You cannot encourage men of decision by confiding the making of decisions to machines, nor create leadership by denying the validity of the life of the mind, nor secure and maintain happiness

[14] "It is exactly this source of creative intuition, often connected with the esthetic, which should interest us—that quality which so clearly distinguishes the great man of business from the mere moneymaker, the statesman from the politician, the truly rational man from the mere dialectician, the scholar from the recorder, and the artist from the reproducer. Strange though it may sound to the modern technical mind, if our schools forget about this intuitive center of the human mind, their instruction, however accurate and diligent, may bury creativeness." Robert Ulich, "The Role of Art in Education," *Art Education Bulletin*, 15 (5):9, May, 1958.

[15] "Let me say then that by 'life-enhancement' I mean the ideated participation in an action, the ideated plunging into a state of being, or state of mind, that makes one feel more hopefully, more zestfully alive; living more intense, more radiant a life not only physically but morally and spiritually as well; reaching out to the topmost peaks of our capacities, contented with no satisfaction lower than the highest." *Aesthetics and History in the Visual Arts*, Pantheon Books, 1948; Anchor Books, 1954, p. 150.

by a vulgar misinterpretation of science. There was a Chinese minister of the eleventh century who, though his reforms were eventually successful, was himself forced out of the emperor's service. One golden sentence of his is as relevant to the problem of the humanities and a national culture now as it was a thousand years ago: "A scholar should be the first to become concerned with this world's troubles and the last to rejoice in its happiness." [16] What Judge Learned Hand puts persuasively in the twentieth century can be approached also from the point of view of a political statesman at the court of a Chinese emperor in 1043, and dead these nine hundred years. The humanities are not mere ornamental parts of a social machine; they give us the embodied political and economic wisdom of the race no less than its aesthetic delights and a record of its sorrow and its merriment.

[16] Quoted in *Chinese Thought and Institutions*, ed. by John K. Fairbank, University of Chicago Press, 1957, p. 111.

2. About Learning and Scholarship

FIVE

The Nature of Learning

It now becomes necessary to discriminate with greater accuracy among some of the terms we have been using. These are:

humanitarian	the humanities
humane	humanist
humanism	humanistic scholarship
humanity	humane learning.

Humanitarian, a quality honorable in itself, we may dismiss as not wholly germane to the problem of learning. *Humane,* when it is a synonym for humanitarian, will likewise go by the board, but not when it refers 1) to a more or less idealized conception of human nature[1] or 2) to the kind of learning supporting this ideal and leading the individual to an increased maturity of outlook. *Humanism,* as we know, originally implied an attitude toward knowledge distinguishing secular learning from theology and denying the claim of theology to superiority, on the ground that the great achievements of classical antiquity were gained without divine revelation.[2] Nowadays hu-

[1] As when John Addington Symonds, having in mind both the idealized quality of the figures in Raphael's paintings and their eternal appeal, says that these paintings are both humane and human.

[2] Humanism may also refer to a quasi-religious doctrine which finds hope for humanity only in the potentialities of the human race for development.

manism sometimes implies all knowledge that leads into self-development. Thus, Walter Lippmann can speak of humanism as the dominant pattern in any program governing the growth of an individual from infancy to self-governing maturity. Modern humanism, moreover, has shed its original hostility to theology. *Humanity* offers no difficulty when it refers to mankind in general. But it may also mean 1) the general state or condition of mankind or 2) the sort of learning supposed to lead mankind into better development. Originally this learning was confined to classical antiquity, and in this sense the word is obsolescent. It is mentioned here because the plural of this noun gives us *the humanities,* or those disciplines[3] with which this book is concerned. A *humanist* is somebody 1) who finds value in the humanities or 2) who accepts the point of view ideally resulting from their study. In the general sense, therefore, anyone is a humanist who maintains a broad, mature, and catholic interest in the actions of men; but in the academic sense a humanist is one who is professionally engaged in interpreting the humanities, usually in the classroom. Like other academic persons he desires to add to knowledge. In this aspect of his work he becomes a humanistic scholar. The aim of *humanistic scholarship* is to increase knowledge in the area of the humanities, and to this subject we shall come in the next chapter. By *humane learning* one refers to that orderly and accurate knowledge of and about the humanities which permits us to interpret them in a clear, consistent, and mature way. This chapter is principally concerned with humane learning.

[3] A discipline is any branch of knowledge acquired through formal study and scholarly research.

2

What is humane learning? Let us begin by briefly noting the relation among humanistic scholarship, humane learning, and the humanities. Just as scientific research aims to increase and refine the body of scientific knowledge, so humanistic scholarship aims to increase and refine humane learning by either adding new facts to what is known, or enriching our knowledge of existing material, or sharpening our understanding of old knowledge by putting it into a new light. The intellectual difference among these three concepts therefore becomes: 1) *humanistic scholarship* produces information that increases what we know about the humanities; 2) *humane learning* fuses this new material with established knowledge and interprets the humanities thus enriched; 3) *the humanities* are those branches of human knowledge (and activity) that have a special capacity, if rightly interpreted by humane learning, to mature the intellectual and moral powers and to quicken the sensibilities of the individual.

Learning is unfortunately an ambiguous word. It may refer merely to rote memory, as when one is made to learn the alphabet; it may mean a conditioned response, as when one says that a dog has learned to ask to come in by scratching at the door; it may signify organized lore in a depreciatory sense, as when one refers to "the learning of the schools"; or it may imply an active, dynamic, and controlled intelligence, well stocked with relevant information and ready to put this information to use in human affairs. This is the ideal of humane learning as the possession of educated men. By convention, moreover, learning in this last sense tends to be referred to learning in nonscientific areas, although learning is as basic to science and the social sciences as it is to the humanities. Nevertheless, we are now to discuss learning in the more restricted sense of knowledge of the humanities.

When animals learn, they submit to training in established routines. Once beyond elementary levels of learning, however, the human being learns through participating in a mental process. By virtue of being human, he possesses human intelligence, and this intelligence is not content with a mere pattern, a mere conditioned response. An active mind looks for meaning beyond the present fact or the present activity. If it didn't, man would never invent anything. It seeks to determine not only what the facts of any situation are but also what will follow from these facts, *i.e.,* what do the facts mean? To answer this question requires study, and study, it is plain, frees the individual from thoughtless enslavement to routine procedures. Study permits man to see the relation between present events and objects and the same events and objects (or like events and objects) in the past and in the probable future. Study implies intelligent choice, the capacity to grasp a variety of potential meanings, explanations, or actions. The human being who comes to grasp this meaning of learning has arrived at individual independence.

Anything and everything within human experience can be made the subject of study, nor is mankind satisfied until it has dealt with everything that has any bearing on human life. Practical needs made the natural environment an early subject for study. Man had to learn enough about things in general to preserve himself, his family, and his tribe. He therefore noted events, he noted recurrences among events, and by and by he arrived at what looked like a general rule apparent in these events, something he could count on amid the accidental, the vague, and the menacing. Science was the wonderful result of this kind of study.

Science became possible when man learned that these

regular occurrences are governed by, or evince, principles that have little or no relation to man's feelings about them. If he is to manage nature at all, he must view natural events and the principles he finds in them with detachment. True, science also puts nature to use, but nature, to be put to use, must be comprehended, and this comprehension must be of nature as it is and not as human desire would prefer nature to be. Effective knowledge of natural processes has to be objective, impersonal, unemotional. The achievement of this attitude by man—one of the great steps forward in human history—did more than give man a workable knowledge of nature; it also emancipated him from the order of mere nature, it released him from the brute pressure of things, it gave him freedom.

The rise of man to human stature is, then, associated with the scientific approach to the natural world. The next great step is implicit in the famous injunction of Socrates: Know thyself. This injunction presupposes a knowledge of nature and an experimental approach to that knowledge, since what Socrates advocated was not random introspection but the reflective use of man's intelligence, once that intelligence had been schooled in and by the natural order. Man must observe himself. But self-observation unchecked by reference to nature and to the conduct of other men, though it may have some personal interest, has very little utility. Not what I want (how do I know what I want?) but what, across the ages and among many cultures and nations, men have learned by experience to want because its satisfactions are lasting—this is the meaning of the injunction of Socrates. To know one's self implies analysis and evaluation of one's desires and impulses, but true evaluation is impossible in terms of the self alone. True evaluation necessarily demands comparison with the conduct and desires of others, with the practicability of such desires and conduct judged by results, in the light of the records of other men's desires and conduct. How do I know that what I want will be either possible or durable? The only possible frame of reference is human experience.

Human experience is recorded in history, it lies about us in society, and at its quintessential best is available in religion, philosophy, and the arts, luminous expressions of man's experiences, his desires, and the possibility of fulfilling his desires. History is the story of what he has done, society is the fact of his present existence, and the arts, philosophy, and religion express his potentialities. Or, not to omit science, we may rephrase this and say that the arts, religion, and philosophy express the possible meanings of life, science discovers meanings in man's confrontation with nature, and the social sciences discover meanings in man's confrontation with other men.

3

But if learning is a basic principle underlying all knowledge, why is the word more closely associated with the humanities than with science and the social sciences? Is the association justified? The humanities would be arrogant indeed if they confined learning to their own field and denied it to the other two. Moreover, a good deal of experience seems to show that learning can also be folly. The learned fool is an unlovely human type, terms like "bookworm" indicate no great reverence for erudition, "academic" often means a pitiable lack of practical experience, and a pedant has no admirers.

Nevertheless, the concept of humane learning, or, to be more specific, the concept of a man of learning carries with it a sense of power. This power arises not only from the fact that any sort of learning is potent because to know something well is to give the knower an inestimable advantage over the ignorant or half-educated man, but it arises also from the very nature of humane studies. We properly feel that the man of learning is never content with the immediate, the popular, the merely useful. He has by study swept over great arcs of time and space, he is aware of issues in history and thought and of the significance of forms of conduct and expression unfamiliar to those who live in present time alone. That is the reason we send our children to sit before him in the college classroom. The experience, we believe, will broaden them. But why and how? The answer is at once simple and grand. The man of learning, and only he, is in potential communion with past greatness—with philosophers and artists and revolutionaries and conservatives, with genius of every order, with the saints and sages of history, with every mighty statement, whether in words, in music, or in the graphic arts, about human destiny that mankind has ever made. He is, however unworthy, an individual member of a great community, of a shadowy but essential priesthood of wisdom; and just as, in religion, the frailty of the server does not affect the efficacy of the sacrament, so it is with learning. The individual voice may be feeble, the particular scholar mediocre, but even the lowliest among learned men has been in some manner touched with fire from the altar. His is the long perspective of time. Whether he deals with vowel changes in Old High German, or the interpretation of Sophocles, or the manuscript of Mozart's *Requiem,* or the significance of the categories of Kant, he symbolizes history. As R. G. Collingwood, the British philosopher-historian, writes:

Historical knowledge is the knowledge of what mind has done in the past, and at the same time it is the redoing of this, the perpetuation of past acts in the present. Its object is therefore not a mere object, something outside the mind which knows it; it is an activity of thought, which can be known only in so far as the knowing mind re-enacts it and knows itself as so doing. To the historian, the activities whose history he is studying are not spectacles to be watched, but experiences to be lived through in his own mind. . . .[4]

That many learned men are mediocre no more alters the greatness of the vocation of the learned man than the mediocrity of thousands of chemists alters the greatness of the scientific ideal.

We have seen that the mind achieves freedom, once it is able to seek out meaning in experience. But meaning is not confined to cause-and-effect relations in the physical world, nor, for that matter, to analyses of social behavior. Nor is meaning confined to economic activities. We do not grow roses merely to sell them, we do not form a collection of music records just to study acoustics, we do not ask of every book we read: "How will this increase my efficiency in the office?" Meaning has another dimension: the dimension of culture.

For an anthropologist, culture means the total habitual ways of a given community. For the humanist, culture refers to only a part, but nevertheless a prepotent part, of these habitual ways. The arts, religion, the philosophic and ethical tradition, the scholarly modes of a community, taken together, develop common traits by communicating to the community and to each other what the community thinks useful to be known. Usefulness here is of a loftier order than bargain and sale. We owe to Aristotle the observation that before there can be learning there must be a community in which a significant number have security and leisure. Security and leisure are not for idleness, but for thought and imagination. By degrees in any community the arts, philosophy, and religion come to embody and express ideal meanings proper to the community, the goals, so to speak, of community imagination, of common

[4] R. G. Collingwood, *The Idea of History*, Oxford University Press, 1946; Galaxy Books, 1956, p. 218.

views and sentiments, and of common values and common faith. The creative arts are among the basic elements in such an expression, both idealizing it and surpassing actuality. So, likewise, philosophy upholds the ethical sentiments of the community, together with religion; and religion, philosophy, and the arts guide education by reminding the community of its goals. Thus, Homer and Hesiod, archaic Greek statuary and the statuary of the Age of Pericles, the thought of the Seven Sages and the thought of Socrates and Plato, the history of Herodotus and the history of Thucydides expressed both a continuing ideal we know as "Greek" and also constantly changing facets of that ideal as the community of Hellas passed through time. The man of learning must be aware both of the constant ideal and of the changing expressions of it.[5]

The study of culture in this high sense is the special domain of learning and of the man of learning. His duty is to interpret for living men the great cultures of the world and to bring to bear upon our present values relevant interpretations of these great cultures. He does this in many ways. He explicates the meaning of a great work of art, or of thought, or of faith. He clarifies the nature of the culture in which the work of art, the religion, or the philosophy developed. He appraises contemporary progress toward the ideal goal of our own culture by indicating where and how we approach, or fail to approach, the greatness of the past and the greatness of our own ideal.

Humane learning is a deliberate attempt at the direc-

[5] ". . . I do not share the now fashionable rejection of philosophical systems. In the progress of humanity systems are necessary because they unify and crystallize our ideas; therefore they emerge usually at a turning point of history. They are like quiet lakes in which men can recognize their faces and the trees around them, but from which also they can set their sails toward new waters. They clarify and elevate man's aspirations; they also serve as foci for new criticism. Of course, great systems are sometimes careless about details; especially, they have not much regard for those who believe their own precious individuality to be at the world's center." Robert Ulich, *The Human Career*, Harper, 1955, p. 241.

tion of culture—of the sentiments and values, the aspirations and hopes of the community in which the man of learning lives. For him the educational process (and his primary aim is, in the Socratic sense, education) must be motivated both by a concern for the community and by a concern for the individual in the community. He judges each by its place in the history of mankind. His concern is not alone for the individual soul but also for the welfare, and even for the survival, of the state. For him the state is not merely here and now; for him the community which the state embodies stretches from the past through the present into the future. The state, if it is to seek and protect the good, must preserve the patrimony of knowledge and enrich that patrimony where it can. The state must therefore, of course, patronize and support science and the social sciences, but if it is to survive, it must also patronize and support the humanities, since the state as a civilized body must embody a humane community, not a mere herd. The state therefore values and enriches humane learning, which is nothing more than man's knowledge of history perpetually reinterpreted, man's knowledge of religion and philosophy perpetually re-examined, and the arts perpetually revalued as statements of wisdom and beauty.[6] The civic responsibility of the man of learning is to preserve the beauty and wisdom of tradition and constantly to draw from this perpetual stream wisdom and beauty appropriate to the present, that is, to the living artist, thinker, philosopher, scientist, housewife, economist, secretary, governor, citizen.

Men seek in vain to do away with the services of the man of learning, proclaiming in one generation that history is bunk, in another that we live in an unprecedented time of peril, in a third that revolution denies or destroys

[6] "The state" here means simply any formal political community, and no question of public versus private education is involved.

history. But in denying history and precedent, the ignorant in fact affirm the social responsibility of the humanities to enlighten them.

The man of learning must exhibit as a matter of course the qualities of all sound intellectual workers, such as openness to ideas, readiness to make inquiry, objectivity (the refusal to sophisticate data by reading into them the private desires of the inquirer or the prejudices of a party), humility of mind, and a capacity to adhere to principles in the cause of truth. Leaving the special study of the natural order to scientists, and of the behavior of men in society to the social scientists, he will not deny that these practitioners of knowledge can be wise and humane persons, but he will quietly insist that his business is also primary. Its primacy lies in the fact that his activity is with the study, inculcation, and absorption of those qualities of mind, character, and spirit (expressed in the arts, philosophy, and religion) which the great cultures of the world have honored as essential alike to individual maturation and to the greatness of the state because they induce responsible social conduct. How? Consider terms like "justice" and "mercy," ideal components of any humane society: the meaning of justice and mercy is to be principally sought in the records of man that are the material of humane learning. So far as "humane" is a point of view, the man of learning will gladly apply this adjective to the scientist and the social scientist when and if they accept and inculcate attitudes and values of maturation, but he will not, therefore, surrender his special role either to science or to social science. The humanities unite the aesthetic world and the moral universe, the world of sensibility and the world of human judgments, not in a didactic fashion, but as vision; and in the light of an ideal vision, compounded out of many elements, the man of learning uniquely fulfills his civic obligation when he strives to shape a good life for the citizen by enabling him to share the concerns of others and mature himself (the inward meaning of "Know thyself"). The man of learning, moreover, will himself strive toward the improvement of the state not by partisanship but by making the fruits of philosophy and works of imagination available to the civic order. The domain of learning was once confined to Greece and Rome. Today the man of learning is no longer content to traffic only in classical antiquity, but, never relinquishing Greece and Rome, he strives through the study of cultures other than those of the Mediterranean world (provided only that these cultures aim at understandable excellence) to bring a comprehension of ways and values not our own into the circle of American life. And always his concern is not for polite learning, not for the aristocratic few, not for didactic programs of betterment. His concern is for Man.

4

This ideal of humane learning and of the man of learning is constantly under attack in America as elsewhere. It is, for example, objected that this ideal is impossible of fulfillment in the United States. Most humanistic scholars, it is said, fail to glimpse or to live by these great notions of obligation and beauty. They have failed to infect most Americans with any such idealism. They have tried to teach foreign languages, and failed. They have not succeeded in teaching literature or philosophy in any real way to the younger generation, and the proof is the linguistic ignorance of the country, a national turning away from reading, the putative shallowness of the national mind. Moreover, even if they succeeded, they would but divert energies more cogent to other questions. Our present problems are with the Russians, with the stock market, with artificial satellites and intercontinental missiles, with the high cost of living, with segregation, with business cycles, with psychiatry.

The objection proves too much. Neither science, nor social science, nor medicine, nor theology lives up to its ideal professions. The lonely voice of a great religious thinker is one thing; the mediocrities that fill the American pulpit are another. The Harvey Cushings of medicine are unique; the run-of-the-mill doctor is always with us. The United States produces now and then a singular genius in the social sciences like Thorstein Veblen, but most economists, most sociologists, most anthropologists are as they are. Humanists sometimes complain that this is the age of science; yet historians also observe that, remarkable as the achievements of applied science in America may be, most original scientific ideas originate somewhere else than in the United States. Nobody therefore suggests giving up the lofty idealism of Christianity, the Hippocratic oath in medicine, the ideal goal of democracy, or the great theoretical aim of science, which is nothing less than the understanding of the total cosmos. Difficult though it is to assess the gap between goal and performance in any field, it would be even more difficult to prove that humane learning is ineffective in the United States to a degree beyond that evident in other forms of human activity.

One can only patiently revert to the traditional ideals of the American republic. We are dedicated to the principle of democratic equality, or the doctrine that every human being has the dignity of being an end in himself. This is precisely the assumption of the humanities and, therefore, the doctrine of humane learning and of the men who profess humane learning. We are dedicated to the principle of liberty, which, whatever else it means, implies the right of the individual to mature on his own inward line of development; and this is precisely what the man of learning finds to be true of the leading spirits of the past. We believe also that the pursuit of happiness is an essential individual right; but happiness, if it have any meaning at all, cannot be ephemeral or delusive. Happiness in this context relates to the permanent satisfactions of life; and it is precisely to the study and evocation of the permanent satisfactions of life that the humanities dedicate themselves and those who profess them. If, moreover, one were to list the American worthies, *i.e.,* those whom the Americans have agreed to honor because they express, each in his own way, the ideal spirit of this republic, one could hardly omit from such a list the names of Franklin, Jefferson, Washington, Lincoln, Lee, and others of like kind. It is not in any way surprising that some of these—Franklin and Jefferson are examples—were virtually professional men of learning, and that all of them exemplified in actuality just those qualities both as private individuals and as responsible citizens that it is the purpose of the man of learning and of the humanities to induce in the lives of their successors as citizens of this same republic. Every profession claims the right to be judged by something better than its failures; and men of learning, in assessing their contribution to the general welfare, claim only the same right they cheerfully accord to religion, medicine, science, and the social sciences. There was only one Greek genius named Socrates, and Athens put him to death, but we continue to judge Athens not by the jury that condemned the philosopher but by the philosopher who died in obedience to the laws of his countrymen.

The books available to Socrates, if, indeed, he owned any, would have been lost in the stacks of a modern university or city library. But as Emerson somewhere remarks, there is no reason to suppose that librarians are wiser than other men. Bookish people are not commonly thought of

as sagacious. On the contrary, Americans have long honored the homely wisdom of the village philosopher, of
whom Franklin was an early, and Will Rogers a later,
incarnation. Untutored men, provided they interpret experience well and have something to guide on, occasionally
confound the learned, as many an anecdote testifies. Experienced scientists sometimes approach quite as close to
angelic wisdom as poets do,[7] and an anthropologist who
has seen all sorts and conditions of men may come closer
to the type of Ulysses than professors of Greek commonly
do—that Ulysses who, in Tennyson's fine poem, declares:

> Much have I seen and known; cities of men
> And manners, climates, councils, governments,
> Myself not least, but honour'd of them all,

and whose spirit yearned

> To follow knowledge like a sinking star
> Beyond the utmost bound of human thought.

It would take an unconscionable amount of brass to declare that simply because he was a man of books, Matthew
Arnold was more philosophical than Thomas Huxley,
Browning wiser than Darwin, or George Meredith profounder than Lord Kelvin. If there is no royal road to
learning, it is also true that the way to wisdom is not necessarily paved with print.

5

Nevertheless, the traditional general belief that the humanities deal in wisdom is sound. This wisdom and this

[7] Consider the splendor of this famous statement by Sir Isaac Newton:
"I do not know what I may appear to the world; but to myself I seem
to have been only like a boy playing on the seashore and diverting myself
in now and then finding a smoother pebble or prettier shell than ordinary,
whilst the great ocean of truth lay all undiscovered before me." Surely
such an utterance meets Dante's test, being *pure e disposto a salire alle
stelle.*

belief must not be perverted into the notion that humanists have some unique monopoly on wisdom, a fallacy that takes shape in the false affirmation that the humanities are concerned with value judgments whereas science and the social sciences are not. The humanities are uniquely concerned with some value judgments—judgments, for example, about what is beautiful and what is banal in art. But the social sciences and science itself are concerned with a basic value judgment (a concern shared by the humanities) expressed in the phrase: You shall know the truth, and the truth shall make you free. Scientist and social scientist by the quality of their lives and their work are excellent examples of the values of patience, humility, and honesty, and the man of learning can but applaud them when they are so and hope to share these shining merits. But he, too, has a contribution to make to wisdom.

On the lowest conceivable plane the man of learning is at least like a roadsign telling people where to go. By the very nature of his calling he is compelled to point to masterpieces of wise thought and art. On the highest plane, since he constantly lives his professional life in the atmosphere of wisdom, greatness, and beauty, it is hard to assume that none of this greatness, this beauty, this wisdom ever rubs off on him. Trafficking as he must in the tradition of Man, he must learn about men and women, whether they be historical personages like Pascal and Montaigne, Goethe and St. Augustine, or imaginary ones like Faustus, Shakespeare's Cleopatra, Mr. Pickwick, Antigone, and the Isaac and Archibald of E. A. Robinson. To deny the possibility that greatness affects the student of greatness is in fact to deny the possibility of really educating anybody. Either we believe in the tradition of humanity or we do not. Our quarrel with learning, and with the man of learning when we do quarrel with him, is in fact a lover's quarrel. Our complaint is not that he fails to traffic in wisdom, our complaint is that he is not Socrates, not Solomon, not Gautama Buddha, so highly do we hold the man of learning in esteem. But if he be not Socrates, he may still have wisdom enough. The town butcher may be, in Victorian terms, a highly respectable man, but as between him and some old teacher, ripe with the experience of twenty or thirty years in the classroom, saturated with the meaning of Shakespeare or Montaigne or Mark Twain or Cicero, the world has rightly leaned to the man of learning. Books ripen readers in ways that those other admirable enterprises the laboratory and the market place cannot. If we did not believe this, we would abolish libraries and put public parks in their place. The man of learning is in a special sense a man of wisdom; and if his wisdom is always more or less faulty, so likewise is the wisdom of the banker, the physicist, the doctor, the businessman, the housewife. Our first feeling about a town without a library and an art gallery is that in such a town life lacks an essential something; our first feeling about a state without learning is that it fails to have essential sagacity. The wisdom of the man of learning is wisdom about Man as he might be, and this is quite as important as his knowledge or lack of knowledge about men as today they are.

SIX

The Nature
of Humanistic Scholarship

At the beginning of the previous chapter we distinguished among several terms concerning the humanities, including *humane learning* and *humanistic scholarship*. We then discussed the theory of humane learning. Let us now turn to its inseparable companion, humanistic scholarship. Humanistic scholarship must be carefully discriminated from humane learning, of which it forms an important component, subsidiary, however, to the total purpose of the humanities. By humanistic scholarship we refer to the specialist's approach to his subject when that subject is some branch of the humanities. Humanistic scholarship stands in relation to humane learning as research work stands in relation to science and social science. Its tools are tools proper to a specialist, its vocabulary the technical vocabulary of the expert. Without humanistic scholarship humane learning could not exist, since learning is the creation of scholarship; and without being continually refreshed from the labors of humanistic scholars humane learning would run dry just as science and the social sciences would grow stale if research were not carried on. Humane learning is, however, a concept superior to the concept of humanistic scholarship in the sense that the function of humane learning is to fuse the results of scholarship into a philosophic outlook and, where necessary, translate the language of scholarship into the general language of culture. But this does not mean that humanistic scholarship is inferior to humane learning as an intellectual activity. The two are related but different. Most laymen and many academic administrators do not understand the nature of this fundamental distinction and are continually disappointed because the humanistic scholar does not per se take on the attributes of the humane man of learning. Professional scholarship and humane interpretation are, or should be, equal and complementary terms, but it confuses the issue to mistake one for the other or to demand of one element in the equation what had better be furnished by the second.

Perhaps the difference in function can be made clear by a metaphor. Let us compare the substance of humane learning to the repertory of a great opera company. The famous figures, the beautiful stage sets, the works of art on the stage, the human story[1]—all these are parts of the drama. The stage is beautifully lighted, the actions are proportionate to the whole, the singers and the chorus perform in succession or harmony, and in the orchestra pit the conductor seems to control, even to create, the total work. But this harmony would not be possible except for the labors of many persons behind the scene and before the curtain rises. The light crew must master the light plot, the scene shifters have to do their chore, the costumers are already at work sewing for the next production, the librarian has distributed their several parts to the orchestra and given a copy of the score to the prompter, and a variety of other labors has to be done before this opera, or its predecessor or its successor, could be staged. We in the audience are conscious only of the beauty and the grandeur of the drama. If the stage crew in their over-

[1] It would strain credibility to call the philosophic discourse proper to humane learning the libretto of the opera!

alls, the prompter in his shirt sleeves, the policeman
guarding the stage door were to intrude upon the stage,
we should feel they had ruined the spectacle. Yet without
these specialists the splendor of the performance could not
have come into being.

If we equate humane learning, with all its repertory of
tragedy and comedy, historic record and present appeal, to
the repertory of our opera company, we can also insist that
humanistic scholars, each working at his special job, are
like the laborers behind the scenes. We do not expect the
stage carpenter to conduct the orchestra, and we should
not expect a scholar who has devoted his life, say, to the
study of the Germanic languages, to write like a philosopher. His excellence lies in the study of philology. Probably he knows more than philology, and we are, of course,
delighted if he show himself to be a philosophic humanist
as well. But the part of wisdom is to realize that the
philologist as scholar has a unique and necessary function
to perform in philology. What he tells us as a specialist we
can eventually weave into the pattern of humane learning.

Humanistic scholars have, then, the right to be judged
in the light of their special tasks, and comment upon them
should be conditioned by the nature of the tasks they do.
These are infinitely varied. Yet there are important general remarks that can be made about all humanistic scholarship—statements that will clarify the nature and value of
this basic activity.

2

The beginning of any humane outlook is human experience. But human experience fades unless it is kept in the
memory or recorded in physical form. The foundation of
the humanities is therefore the records of human life. In
most cases these records are tangible, physical objects in

the external world. In some cultures, of course, records were memorized and passed from one generation of record-keepers (usually priests) to another by word of mouth. Moreover, in many cultures oral tradition is the mode by which legend and custom, myth and folklore have been preserved and transmitted to posterity, and, of course, all the languages of the world pass from one generation to another by oral communication and imitation—literally, by word of mouth. Oral tradition is intangible and not a physical object. Yet the diligence of scholars is such that oral tradition, so to speak, can be made to shrink as its contents are recorded on tape or in type. Languages that have no written alphabet can be recorded and studied by linguistic specialists.[2]

In addition, certain of the arts—oratory, playing music, singing, and the dance are examples—offer special difficulties in the matter of their records, and these difficulties have until recent times placed them in the category of tradition. The motion picture, the phonograph, the wire recorder, and like machines now permit us to preserve the actual sounds and movements of celebrated practitioners of these arts. Enrico Caruso, Charlie Chaplin, and Sir Winston Churchill have been recorded for posterity as Mario, David Garrick, and William Pitt were not. Since, until the twentieth century, there was no way of recording creation and performance, no matter how persuasive the speaker, how moving the musical execution, or how beautiful the dance, all that we have concerning great personalities of the past in this regard is records or stories *about* the artist or the speaker. We do not have a record *of* the artist or the speaker.

Despite this truth and although the tooth of time constantly gnaws at everything man makes and keeps, it is

[2] Contrariwise, languages no longer spoken, such as the hieroglyphics of ancient Egypt or the cuneiform records found in Mesopotamia can be studied. Ancient Greek and classical Latin fall virtually into this category.

upon the more nearly permanent monuments[3] of culture that the humanities depend for their existence. These monuments humanists labor to preserve, understand, and interpret to their fellow men. The humanistic scholar is, in the intellectual order, the first to undertake this task.

Monuments fall into two great classes: things (as, for example, an Indian arrowhead); and words or signs (the manuscripts of Haydn's symphonies are an instance). Among archaeologists things of human manufacture, usually small, which help the scholar to interpret the culture that produced them, come to be known as *artifacts*, and though this word does not commonly apply to great paintings or other art forms of major importance, for the purpose of the present analysis let us agree to call physical things of interest to humanistic scholarship by this word. Words or signs of similar interest we shall call *documents*. Humanistic scholarship deals with artifacts, whether they be hairpins from ancient Egypt or the statuary of Barlach, and with documents, by which we shall understand discourse, written, carved, or otherwise recorded (as on a tape). A document carries with it some intention of permanence. Documents may be the latest novel, the text of a political treaty, the Rosetta stone, a Buddhist prayer, stenographic writing (as in the case of Pepys's diary), the morning newspaper (already become history), a cancelled check, and the like. But wherever the artifact or the document holds or can be made to reveal some record of human life of more than ephemeral value,[4] there the humanistic

---

[3] "Monuments" probably calls up the image of a graveyard, in which, it is alleged, humanists and humanistic scholars spend too much time. The word is used here in a sense more nearly in accord with its root meaning (Latin, *monere,* to remind). Monuments here mean works, sayings, deeds, and creations worthy of enduring through some long space of time.

[4] Lapse of time may turn ephemera into artifacts or documents of considerable value. Most bank statements, having served a temporary purpose, are thrown away. Could we, however, recover Shakespeare's bank state-

scholar can go to work. By "some record of human life" one does not refer to "history" only. The "Mona Lisa" of da Vinci is, for this purpose, as much a record of human life as are the records of the trial of Charlotte Corday, who murdered Marat in his bath in Paris in 1793.

If artifact and document are to yield their full values to successive generations of men and in varying cultures, it is evident they must be exposed to at least five processes:

1. The artifacts and the documents must be discovered.

2. They must be identified.

3. They must be preserved and, if possible, duplicated both as a precaution against loss and as a means of widening their study.

4. They must be studied until they are understood by specialists versed in the knowledge of the time, place, and conditions that produced them, and versed also in the knowledge of the antecedents and consequences of the artifacts and documents; and they must also be understood by at least a minority in the culture supporting the humane learning in which the study is carried on.

5. They must be ever and again rescanned for new understanding, new meanings, and new relevances or applications to present culture.

Humanistic scholarship is concerned in all five of these stages. The first and second phases are almost wholly in the province of humanistic scholarship. The third—that of preservation and duplication—is of vital concern to the humanistic scholar, but also involves such allied specialists as the librarian, the archivist, the museum director, and the printer (or other duplicator), and perhaps the translator. The humanistic scholar is obviously central in the fourth stage, but this responsibility he shares with the man of learning in the latter's capacity as interpreter, teacher,

ments, or, rather, their equivalents, how interested we would all immediately be!

expositor, or critic.[5] These various phases of humane learning, or, rather, the practitioners of these various modes of
discovering, evaluating, and interpreting the substance of
the humanities, are not separate, or at least ought not to
exist each by itself. The humanistic scholar must know
the general frame of reference in which his research has
meaning, the interpreter-teacher must likewise be a scholar,
the critic must possess himself of relevant historical knowledge of what he interprets, and the man of learning, who
may in some sense exemplify all these "concerns," tries to
understand each interest and each point of view involved.
But our "concern" for the moment is with the humanistic
scholar.

By common consent (and, of course, for better and more
philosophical reasons also) the great monuments of human
culture—Homer, the Parthenon, Newton's *Principia,* the
music of Mozart, the work of Goya, Dickens's novels, the
mosaics in Santa Sophia, the Bible, and so on—are the

[5] How important it is to understand an accepted document both in
terms of the culture that produced it and in terms of its meaning to
present-day society is evident in a simple instance recently studied by
scholars: The American Constitution was written in the eighteenth century by men of the eighteenth century, using an eighteenth-century
vocabulary with eighteenth-century meanings. One word in that vocabulary was "commerce." The "commerce clause" of the Constitution gives
the Congress power "to regulate commerce with foreign nations, and
among the several States, and with the Indian tribes." "Commerce" in the
eighteenth century meant in this context little more than trade and
barter; yet upon this original simple concept the vast structure of federal
regulation of trade has been reared. The labors of the linguist and of the
historian of political theory unite in a problem of interpretation like this
with the special learning of law and political science, including knowledge
of the administrative process.

Another instance of somewhat indirect interest to Americans is this:
Enthusiasts have traced the "liberties of Englishmen" backward to Magna
Charta (1215). Modern scholarship points out that Magna Charta was
rather more in the nature of a contract or treaty between King John and
his chief barons about the demands the king might make on the barons
and the barons, in turn, on their vassals than it was a declaration of
rights such as the French "Declaration of the Rights of Man," and that
the word "liberty" (or, rather, its equivalent in Medieval Latin) scarcely
meant what the word means today.

occasions of scholarly investigation and interpretation. Thus specialists have for decades patiently tried to piece together bits of evidence about Mayan civilization. Every generation adds something either to our knowledge of Shakespeare or to new, valid, and fruitful ways of interpreting what he wrote. When the concern of humanistic scholarship is with great personalities, great works of art, or great problems like the nature of Mayan civilization, the public mind is prepared to acquiesce at least in the desirability of scholarship. But when the scholar demands for his professional happiness a complete collection of third-rate fiction of the eighteenth century, or when he puzzles over the burned edges of the solitary *Beowulf* manuscript, or when he writes about verbs of eating or drinking in Old High German, or when he quarrels about the authenticity of a picture attributed to the school of Leonardo da Vinci, opinion changes, and the layman begins to question the validity of humanistic research. Adjectives like "antiquarian," "pedantic," "irrelevant," or "futile" then appear in educational discussion. Can anything be said concerning the importance that scholarship imputes to artifact or document as part of its materials?

The importance of document or artifact varies according to its relevance to the problem before the scholar, and this in turn may vary according to the needs or values of the culture in which humanistic scholarship is active at the time. Obviously the score of a symphony by Shostakovich is of more "importance" for contemporary musical culture than the recording of a popular song on the "Hit Parade"—unless, of course, inquiry is being made into the significance for culture of popular songs. On the other hand, more scholarship has been expended on the history of "Dixie" and its composer than has gone into studying pretentious but now forgotten compositions contemporary with Dan Emmett. For example, Michael Balfe's opera

The Siege of Rochelle was "rapturously received" at Drury Lane in 1835, but musicology has virtually no interest today in the pallid score of a pallid opera. Again: most wills interest only the immediate family, but specialists have pored over the text of Shakespeare's will, trying to infer from it the personality of Shakespeare.[6] Riddles appear weekly in the children's page of the newspaper, but a whole subdepartment of Old English scholarship concerns Anglo-Saxon riddles. Context often determines importance.

Other general statements can be made. The value of artifact or document may increase in proportion as other evidence is scanty. Many a modern soldier has scratched his initials on his mess kit, a fact of no interest to anybody else except his sergeant, but scholarship carefully deciphers names appearing in runes on a couple of metal pieces called chapes covering the hook or catch by which a scabbard was attached to the belts of two swordsmen long dead. These relics, found in Thorsbjaerg, date from the third or fourth century, the names are Germanic, and deciphering them was like striking a match in a dark room: we learn what sort of people presumably lived in Schleswig seventeen hundred years ago.

Clearly, also, artifact or document of no intrinsic value may prove matter of great moment in association with something else. For example, in mid-nineteenth-century Italy Robert Browning casually picked up from a bookstall the bound records of a murder trial centuries old. This formed the basis of his masterpiece, *The Ring and the Book,* in which he retells the story from ten[7] separate points of view, insisting that throughout these reinterpretations he has adhered strictly to the facts of the rec-

---

[6] And also the social status of a testator who leaves his "second best bed with the furniture" to his wife.

[7] There are twelve books, but Guido and Browning speak twice.

ords. The records, now in print as *The Old Yellow Book,* are available to humanistic scholarship. To study them is, in the first place, to enjoy an illuminating lesson in the way a great artist shapes raw material into a masterpiece; and, in the second place, to learn that Browning was not quite candid in saying he had altered nothing. On the contrary, he altered a great deal. His heroine, the saintly Pompilia, for example, is not the shrewd little peasant girl of the records. No one pretends that *The Old Yellow Book*[8] has much value per se, but its existence throws light on the process by which Browning transmutes the "dross" of the records into the "gold" of poetry and also poses important questions about the difference between truth of fact and truth of art.

Another principle should be remembered; namely, that the accumulation of small items, each of small value, may lead to important discoveries. Thus, archaeologists, assuming from the Bible and from classical literature that the kingdoms of Assyria and Babylonia were the principal historical powers of Mesopotamia, accumulated a vast amount of clay tablets with cuneiform inscriptions, some of which they could decipher and some of which puzzled them. Years went by. Scholars then discovered in western Persia the "Rock of Behistun" with cuneiform inscriptions in three languages, and, proceeding (as in the case of the Rosetta stone) from the languages they could decipher to the one that had hitherto baffled them, stumbled upon a "new" language, Sumerian, learned that the Assyrians had borrowed cuneiform writing from the Sumerians, and thus opened the door upon a vast and exciting chapter of history—the story of a culture that produced a democratic

---

[8] See in this connection the edition of *The Old Yellow Book,* tr. by J. M. Gest, Chipman Law Pub. Co., 1925; F. T. Russell, *One Word More on Browning,* Stanford University Press, 1927; and J. E. Shaw, "The 'Donna Angelica' in *The Ring and the Book,*" *PMLA,* 41:55–81, March, 1926.

state older than Athens.[9] Bit by bit, brick tablets yielded
their story. Again: folklorists have for years been collecting
American Indian (Amerindian) folk tales, each of which
has a certain charm. Two social psychologists, who have
had experience interpreting "original" (imaginative) stories by children and teen-agers, turn to these collections of
folk stories, analyze them from their point of view, and
find there examples of "modal motivation" of members of
the culture producing these stories. The tales suggest, they
say, "that cultures which are concerned with achievement
are likely to stress independence training in childhood,
which in turn produces a higher level of achievement
motivation in members of the culture. . . ." [10] Thus a
new insight into modes of understanding human behavior
is born.

The first duty of the humanistic scholar, if he is going to
enrich knowledge, is to discover and identify documents
and artifacts relevant to his task. If he is to fulfill his task,
he must know where to look for these materials, but he
will not know where to look unless his professional education has taught him how to go about looking—where to
hunt, how to identify the object when he finds it, how to
distinguish between genuine and spurious material, how
to be sure the artifact or the document has been cleared of
all matter that does not belong to it. Then, and only then,
can he interpret what he has found.

The problem of where to look requires specialized historical training, commonly, though not only, given in our
graduate schools. That is, the young scholar must not only

[9] See the fascinating article "The Sumerians" by Professor Samuel Noah
Kramer of the University of Pennsylvania, in the *Scientific American* for
October, 1957, pp. 71 ff., with its valuable illustrations.

[10] David C. McClelland and G. A. Friedman, "A Cross-Cultural Study
of the Relationship between Child-Training Practices and Achievement
Motivation Appearing in Folk Tales," in *Readings in Social Psychology*,
ed. by Guy E. Swanson *et al.*, Holt, 1952, pp. 243 f. See also *The Achievement Motive* by McClelland *et al.*, Appleton, 1953.

know enough not to look for Dead Sea scrolls in Iceland
or cuneiform bricks in Arizona, he must also learn where
collections of manuscripts are housed, what libraries and
museums specialize in this or that period or culture, what
official bureaus contain what sort of official documents,
what series of printed works exist, what books by what
authorities are to be consulted, and what the latest word is
from the intellectual frontier in this area. He must also
master the languages necessary for him to read materials
relevant to his problem. The better the training given the
young scholar in this respect, the better his scholarship is
likely to be. Attempts to shorten or lighten the burden of
professional education have been made, but below a certain minimum of accomplishment graduate work cannot
fall if it is to maintain effective scholarship.

But this is not all. Steps two, three, and four in research
work involve identifying the object, distinguishing what is
genuine from what is spurious among objects (or in a given
object, whether document or artifact), and clearing the
artifact or the document of what does not belong to it,
skills that require further training in the craft of scholarship. In the world of artifacts this means the ability to distinguish among styles and periods, so that the young
scholar will not confuse ornamentation on a Greek vase of
one period with that of a later period and so misinterpret
evidence. Distinguishing spurious work from genuine production also turns upon this mastery of style, both in the
sense of an authoritative "feeling" for style and period and
in the sense of mastering the elements that make up the
style under examination. Forgery seems to have a constant
allure for the human race and is a problem in scholarship
whether it concern the Piltdown skull or rare nineteenth-
century pamphlets, the famous "Donation of Constantine"
or the infamous Protocols of the Elders of Zion. The ideal
of scholarship must forever be the ideal of all scientific

work: scrupulous adherence to truth. That is, the artifact must be genuine, the text of the document must be what the author wrote and not what other (and later) people wanted to make him write. Scholarly training means education in "the habit of truth," identical with truth of science:

The scientific method and outlook go back to one principle: that each man has the single responsibility to seek the truth (empirical and rational), to acknowledge it and to act on it. The cleavage today is not between materialism and high-mindedness; on the contrary, it is between the truth-seeking spirit and the lip-service to conventional absolutes. . . . The scientist undertakes not to deceive even himself (and no matter for what good end) in the most minute detail of procedure—a wave length, a speck in a culture of bacteria, the failure of the remotest consequence of his theory to accord with fact. This homogeneity of outlook, this unity of belief with action, marks the scientific mind. . . .[11]

Substitute "scholarly" for "scientific" in this passage, and the implied injunction remains valid.

3

It is well to linger for a moment on the grueling disciplines to which the humanistic scholar must ever and again subject himself. We have said that his training begins in the graduate school; we add that it never ends. He never knows what he may be called upon to do next, for the reason that, document and artifact being the products of men, any facet of human life may be expressed by them and any form of knowledge may be necessary to their interpretation. He may be called upon to decipher an un-

[11] Jacob Bronowski in *The Nation,* July 14, 1956, pp. 41–42. The phrase "habit of truth" is borrowed from the second chapter of his little book *Science and Human Values,* Messner, 1956.

known tongue, as Jean François Champollion deciphered
Egyptian hieroglyphics, or to master "dead" languages in
order to distinguish between the Greek of the Alexandrian
Age and the Greek of the tenth century, or to devise a
system of recording a language never written down. He
may have to master statistical method if he is involved in
word counts proper to an analysis of style or to the best
modes of learning foreign languages. He may have to learn
enough chemistry to distinguish among varnishes if the
ascription of a painting is involved, and he may borrow
from the physicist scintillation counters if he has to determine the age of a piece of cloth from a tomb. He learns to
recognize not only the kinds of mistakes scribes commit in
copying manuscripts in medieval monasteries, but also the
kinds of errors printers make in "setting up" copy, whether
in Caxton's time or in that of John Murray. He may have
to learn the history of psychological theory if he is to
determine the motives of Shakespeare's plays or make
credible the effects of embracing Christianity in the novels
of James Fenimore Cooper. He studies theology to understand Milton, ancient science to understand Lucretius,
medieval cosmogony to understand Dante. He must draw
upon the history or the conventions of perspective if he is
to distinguish what Paolo Uccello, Marcel Duchamp, and
Ma Yüan were painting in their respective times and
countries. Interpreting texts, he must be careful not to
read modern meanings into words used in a sense now
obsolete, not to leave the modern reader helpless where
the text seems nonsensical or absurd, and not to pretend
knowledge where he has none.[12] Of course, not all scholars

[12] Here are examples of each of these three. When in his "Elegy Written
in a Country Churchyard" Gray writes: "Can honor's voice *provoke* the
silent dust?" he does not mean *irritate,* but *call forth.* When Dante says
he went *"dove il sole* tace" (where the sun is silent), he does not mean
that the sun stopped talking, he means he went where the harmony of
the spheres was inaudible. When, in *Antony and Cleopatra,* the messen-

have to acquire all these "disciplines," but the point is that scholarly training is, and must be, as rigorous as the training of the scientist or the social scientist, the demands upon the scholar are quite as enormous, and the opportunities of scholarship quite as vast. Summing up seventeen chapter-length statements about the progress of knowledge in a variety of fields having to do with man, the editor of *Frontiers of Knowledge* remarks that this survey of disciplined scholarship "announces not the ideal but the fact of a new kind of humanism: a humanism stripped of provincialism and preciosity, one no longer bound by an exclusive concern for the Western tradition of culture or by the interests of an aristocratic society." [13] But this increase of perspective, if it exists, merely underlines the truth that scholarly training, like training in medicine, law, or any other profession, increases its demands upon the practitioner, it does not diminish them, sentimental desires to the contrary notwithstanding.

4

Having completed a research task and having formulated his conclusions, the humanistic scholar has next the duty of making available to his peers what he has found out. Scholars are his immediate, his primary audience. They, and they alone, will know without elaborate exposition the context of the problem he has tried to solve. He therefore puts his discoveries and conclusions into words, diagrams, or pictures, or some combination of these, writing

ger describes Antony's departure to Cleopatra, he says that Antony "soberly did mount an *arm-gaunt* steed." After citing several pages of explanation of this cryptic compound, the editor of the Variorum Edition of Shakespeare quite properly observes that neither he nor anybody else really knows what it means, however much it may add to our appreciation of Antony's courage in mounting so mysterious an animal.

[13] *Frontiers of Knowledge in the Study of Man*, ed. by Lynn White, Jr., Harper, 1956, p. xii.

an article directed to other experts in order to induce comment, criticism, and acceptance of what he has found. Sometimes publication is preceded by the oral presentation of his paper to a learned gathering, and sometimes publication is postponed until he has accumulated enough other relevant material to make a monograph, that is, an exhaustive treatment in book form of his problem. Commonly, however, the learned article is the first statement of his research work. This article he sends to an appropriate learned journal.

Every field of learning or of science has one or more specialized journals for the diffusion of the results of research among scholars. Such journals do not appeal to the general reader for support—indeed, they are not supposed to do so. They are edited, written, and in some sense published by scholars for scholars. The editors usually receive no pay, nor are the contributors commonly paid, for the assumption is that the work of each is part of his professional labor as a scholar. Obviously such periodicals characteristically enjoy only a small circulation, especially when this is compared to the circulation of the "mass media" or even of such general magazines as the *Atlantic* or *Harper's*. Circulations of two, three, and four hundred are not uncommon, the subscribers to such journals being academic libraries, museums and institutes here and abroad, and a sprinkling of scholars over the world. Nevertheless, precisely as the humanities are to be understood only in a context of humane learning, and as humane learning stales without the refreshment of new insights, new values, and new information gained from research, so research would remain virtually inaccessible even among professional scholars were it not for the scholarly journals. This is not to deny grave defects among these publications: they are often begun too rashly, they are sometimes slackly edited, their contents are occasionally trivial, and the theory and practice of scholarly writing need improvement. But improvements must work in the direction of enriching scholarship, not in some other direction, such as edification or pedagogy. *The scholarly journal is a quintessential part of all sound humanistic life and requires to be supported as such.*

The next stage in the development of the scholar, and often the mark of his maturation, is the creation of a book of major import. That book may be a monograph—an exhaustive discussion, presumably authoritative, of some lesser phase of his great field—or it may be a treatise, such as Wylie Sypher's *Four Stages of Renaissance Style,* Richard Chase's *The American Novel and Its Tradition,* René Wellek's *A History of Modern Criticism: 1750–1950,* C. I. Lewis's *The Ground and Nature of the Right,* or John Hope Franklin's *From Slavery to Freedom,* each of which is an authoritative discussion of a major cultural issue: the evolution of styles in the arts, the qualities of American fiction, the development of an understanding of values in literature, the relation between reason and ethics, and the story of the Negro in America. The distinction between a monograph and a treatise is not easy to draw. It is not a question of length—some monographs are longer than general books or treatises. But in a monograph the scholar is commonly addressing an audience of scholars on a particularized topic, whereas in a treatise the scholar hopefully approaches to the condition of a man of learning and seeks to address not only an audience of specialists but a cultivated and intelligent general public as well. Thus, in *The Political Philosophy of Hobbes,* the German scholar Leo Strauss tries to bring together in a single book of less than two hundred pages all that can be said about a single phase of the thought of a single philosopher. This close study, this careful and detailed dissection of Hobbes's thought will inevitably be of more interest to students of political theory and of philosophy than to anybody else.

But in *The Classical Tradition* Gilbert Highet undertakes to inform any cultivated reader about the relations between the classical past and cultural epochs subsequent to the "fall of Rome." A mature scholar may, of course, produce a monograph, but the younger scholar seldom has the information, the experience, or the maturity to produce a treatise.

Scholars also produce other kinds of writing—book reviews, textbooks, edited texts for classroom purposes, and so on. But the crown of a scholarly career is commonly thought to be a treatise of such weight and dignity that its appearance marks an epoch in the development of interpretation in a field of learning. Such a book was *The Drama of the Medieval Church* by Karl Young, an example from literary history, the product not merely of fine and subtle scholarship but also of mature reflection upon the nature of dramatic art. Other instances of definitive works can be selected from almost any field of humanistic scholarship, including the social humanities—books like James G. Frazer's *The Golden Bough*, Sir Henry Maine's *Ancient Law*, Arthur E. Haigh's *The Attic Theatre*, Henry Adams's *History of the United States, 1801–1817*, Alexander W. Thayer's *Life of Ludwig van Beethoven*, Harry A. Wolfson's *Philo*, Jakob C. Burckhardt's *Civilization of the Renaissance in Italy*, Leslie Stephen's *History of English Thought in the Eighteenth Century*. Works like these and scores of others are turning points in the history of thought and, therefore, of culture. In such masterpieces the specialist melts into the scholar, the scholar into the man of learning.

SEVEN

Achievements in Scholarship

By their very nature humanistic scholars cannot stage such dramatic events as the dropping of a bomb on Hiroshima or the launching of an artificial satellite, nor do they commonly produce such obvious successes as a vaccine against polio, the Keynesian theory of economics, tranquilizing drugs, or a Hoover report on government efficiency.[1] Occasionally, of course, striking episodes connected with scholarship get into the newspapers, as when somebody opens a seventeenth-century grave in the hope of determining the authorship of the Shakespeare plays. The humanistic scholar is not necessarily a shrinking violet, but events like this, or, rather, the publicity they receive, embarrass him by throwing a false light on scholarship. He thinks the march of mind in scholarship is not measurable by publicity. He may be wrong, but publicity is a function of journalism, not of research. Certainly, however, the absence of general knowledge about the more ordinary life and growth of scholarship has inevitably led to doubt among laymen concerning the vigor and use of scholarly activities. Is the humanistic scholar anything more than an

---

[1] Success here means immediate attention and possible influence; it is not argued that these discoveries, inventions, or findings are successful immediately and invariably.

118

antiquarian? [2] How far is the charge of lack of progress just?

Let us glance, however superficially, at humane learning and try to discover what, if anything, has been happening of importance in this vast area in the United States during the last fifty or sixty years. We shall have, of course, to waive the philosophical problem of what is meant by "progress," but we can note change at least. Nor can we always distinguish between world scholarship and purely American work.

We begin by noting that information in all areas of knowledge has increased at a faster rate since 1900 than in any other fifty or sixty years in all recorded time. The material on which scholarship is exercised has cumulated, if not with the frightening rapidity of expansion in the sciences, to an almost unmanageable degree, nevertheless. We know more, and know more about more, languages than was true in Victoria's day. Information in every field of art has multiplied prodigiously, and, in addition, a bewildering variety of new forms of art has matured—the "modern" ballet (after 1907), the motion picture, drama for radio,[3] jazz as "serious" music,[4] the twelve-tone technique,

[2] The fortunes of this word and of its cognate, "antiquarianism," in American English are interesting. "Antiquarianism" had the original meaning of a faithful, patient, and sympathetic study of artifacts and documents descending to us from any remote period of time. Neither Webster's unabridged dictionary of 1953 nor Roget's famous thesaurus recognizes "antiquarianism" in its pejorative or "smear word" sense. This meaning seems to have arisen out of recent educational discussion characterized more by emotion than by understanding. It is amusing to note that similar charges of antiquarianism are not now leveled against scientists and social scientists, but were so leveled as late as *Gulliver's Travels* (1726), where they appear as "projectors." Read the account of Laputa in Book III.

[3] Striking examples are Orson Welles's famous broadcast about a Martian invasion, and "The Fall of the City" by Archibald MacLeish.

[4] George Gershwin's *Rhapsody in Blue* and *Porgy and Bess* come immediately to mind.

musique concrète, new modes of statuary, surrealistic painting, collage, photomontage, literature as free association,[5] and so on. Each of these new forms has a history, theory, philosophy, and aesthetic of its own that scholarship struggles to master. In the same period, moreover, methods of duplicating material have multiplied—carbon copies, photography, offset printing, mimeographing, multigraphing, microfilming, new methods in color reproduction, new ways of duplicating statues, new processes for making lantern slides, and, of course, motion pictures. If these inventions have made more material quickly available to scholars, they have also increased the burden of scholarship by increasing the bulk of matter to be searched. The single field of history, however defined, has taken on the qualities of a gigantic nightmare. Not only do we know more prehistory and protohistory than Henry Adams did, but the area of ancient history has grown to include empires the last century never heard of. The obligations of living in One World have thrown upon the historians the burden of assimilating the histories of both ancient and modern Oriental cultures. The contemporary era is itself so historically self-conscious that it preserves its own records in unprecedented fullness, to the embarrassment of scholars, who have not yet digested the records of World War I. A new sense of the significance of neglected elements in the story of man has led to the creation of new scholarly associations like the History of Science Society, and new modes of collecting materials have increased the opportunities and the burdens of associations like the American Folklore Society and the American Musicological Society. Finally, despite martial interruptions, the

---

[5] Contrast the structure, meaning, and style of Tennyson's "Ulysses" with that of T. S. Eliot's *The Waste Land,* and Goethe's *Faust* with the "unanimist" poetry of Conrad Aiken. The prose of Gertrude Stein and James Joyce, and William Faulkner in *The Sound and the Fury* would have been impossible prior to Freud.

international connections of scholarship steadily increase as associations from UNESCO to the Union Académique Internationale, and meetings ranging from an International Congress of Papyrology to the International Congress of Philosophy, made possible by air travel, call scholars together from the four quarters of the globe.[6]

During the first half of the twentieth century scholarship has succeeded in rewriting every leading encyclopedia in the Western world, and sometimes in rewriting them two or three times. In 1928 it brought to completion the Oxford New English Dictionary, the greatest dictionary of the language ever published, and it has also revised every other leading English dictionary. Similar achievements mark the principal foreign languages. American scholarship also produced such excellent compilations as the one-volume Columbia Encyclopaedia and innumerable useful guides typified by the *Harvard Guide to American History*. It created the Encyclopaedia of the Social Sciences (1930–35) in fifteen volumes and the *Dictionary of American Biography* in twenty-two. It is presently helping other great enterprises, international in character, such as the *Codices Latini Antiquiores,* the *Corpus Vasorum Antiquorum,* the *Corpus Vitrearum Medii Aevi,* an Assyrian dictionary, the *Monumenta Musicae Byzantinae,* and an archive of Islamic culture. If these seem too remote for human nature's daily food, consider J. D. Hart's *Oxford Companion to American Literature,* revised, in one volume, the *Literary History of the United States* in three, Frank Luther Mott's *History of American Magazines,* still unfinished, in four, W. A. Craigie's *Dictionary of American English on Historical Principles* in four volumes, and

[6] A gathering like the Royal Anthropological Institute Symposium on "The Artist in Tribal Society," held in London in October, 1957, would have been impracticable before transatlantic air travel became commonplace.

M. M. Mathews' *Dictionary of Americanisms on Historical Principles* in two.

2

Let us next examine particular areas of humanistic scholarship, beginning with language, that large and generous word. To most of us the study of "language" connotes the mastering of English, and some acquaintance with (and possible command of) one or more modern foreign languages. Logically the "dead" languages also come under this rubric. Certainly here are worthy aims. The teaching of foreign languages has been a major educational enterprise in the United States for many decades, and nobody need be surprised if the problems it creates are not yet satisfactorily solved. Although contemporary scholarship and contemporary engineering aid teaching by creating new mechanical devices like phonograph records and tape recordings and unusual patterns of instruction like the use of a native "informant," we have still a long way to go. Recently there has been a resurgence of interest in more efficient methods of instruction involving a revival of devices employed as early as World War I and arising also from the application of genuinely new information about the nature of language. One of the achievements of the twentieth century has been the increased availability of materials for the learning of Oriental languages and a growing sense of their importance. Still, when one considers the number of Japanese who learn English in contrast to the number of Americans who learn Japanese, the comparison is not flattering.

But practical aims and applications, no matter how important, are not our present concern.[7] Rather, we must

[7] This is not to shrug the problem off. For a survey of the history and present state of modern foreign-language teaching see the Anniversary

deal with recent developments in the humanistic and scientific understanding of language as a basic aspect of human behavior. It seems fair to say that the last fifty years have seen a virtual revolution in the field. "Language" nowadays includes linguistics, philology, communication, semantics, and a philosophy, or philosophies, of meaning, and is being studied by the engineer, the metaphysician, the medical man, the psychologist, and the cultural historian no less than by the specialist we call the philologian —who has, in the same interval, developed new specialties and approaches all his own.

Although a philosophic concern with certain aspects of language, particularly grammar and rhetoric, has been of ancient concern in our Western tradition, a scientific approach arose only rather late in the eighteenth century. Then, and during much of the nineteenth century, the overriding motif in all manner of scholarly activity was the genetic approach, or historicism. What could not be explained as a phenomenon of the present became clear and understandable, it was thought, when it was viewed in proper historical perspective, sometimes real, sometimes invented for the purpose. This historicism long governed the investigations of philologians; and all that the influence of Darwin did for a time was to change historicism into evolutionism. Accordingly, our twentieth-century inheritance was very largely what is called *historical linguistics:* the theory of the mechanisms by which the design of

Issue of the *Modern Language Journal,* XL (6), October, 1956, especially the articles by Henry Grattan Doyle and Henri Peyre. For accounts of the latest campaign to encourage foreign-language teaching see the reports on "The F. L. Program" written by the staff of the Modern Language Association and printed and distributed by D. C. Heath and Co. Report No. 2, for instance, discusses the qualifications necessary for secondary-school teachers of modern foreign languages. On the general program and problem consult *The National Interest and Foreign Languages,* a discussion guide prepared by William Riley Parker and sponsored by the United States National Commission for UNESCO, rev. ed., January, 1957, Department of State Publication 6389, Washington, D. C.

a language changes with the passage of time and partly because of the passage of time; the ways in which languages influence each other; and, through the comparative method, the analysis of related languages so that a rather accurate picture of their common ancestor can gradually be worked out.

"Synchronic" studies—that is, investigations aimed at understanding and describing how a language works at any particular time—were not neglected in the nineteenth century, but apart from a few excellent descriptions of specific languages (for example, Samuel Kleinschmidt's study of Greenlandic), most such work was more distinguished for philosophical or pseudo-philosophical speculation than by a hardheaded, scientific point of view. Slowly a more objective and less speculative synchronic method in linguistics has emerged. It was first carried forward from about 1890 to about 1940 by scholars like August Leskien, Ferdinand de Saussure, Franz Boas, Edward Sapir, Leonard Bloomfield, and N. S. Trubetzkoy. A significant fraction of the nineteenth-century historical view has been set aside as wrong. The study of the history of a language is one task, the study of how a language "works" at any given time is another. Techniques are now available whereby an investigator can approach a language he knows nothing about in advance save that it is a language, and yet dissect and describe it. We know far more today about the elements that are common to all human languages—the basic ground plan, as it were, without which a system of communication is not a human language but something else. Scholarship today is aware of the enormous extent to which whatever a person says at a given moment is determined by his linguistic and cultural heritage, the surprisingly small extent to which what he says stems from "free choice." We begin to discern the ways in which the language of a community crisscrosses ("anastomoses" is the appropriate medical term) with the rest of its culture, each conditioning the other. Modern linguistic science is both a behavioral science and one of the humanities. Its methods of investigation are strongly suffused with the contemporary scientific world view. But the fact that so many kinds of experts are concerned about language is a tribute to the fundamental importance of language in human life.

In American scholarship perhaps the formation of the Linguistic Society of America in 1924 is a significant date. Its first meeting was addressed by Leonard Bloomfield, called by one enthusiast "probably the most influential single personality" in linguistic studies in the country. He announced that the "science of language, dealing with the most basic and simplest of human institutions, is a human science" and declared that "the needs of society make it the duty of students of language to work together systematically, and with that sense of craftsmanship and of obligation which is called professional consciousness." The key ideas are that there *is* a science of language, that this science may be systematically pursued, and that linguistic nationalism is not a proper division of linguistic learning. The work of this society and of other groups like it has enabled the contemporary specialist not only to know far more than did his nineteenth-century predecessor in the field, but also to render far greater practical service to psychologists, government, engineers, business, industry, education, literary criticism, and archaeology than was dreamed of in 1900.[8]

[8] For a brief overview of present linguistic knowledge see the chapter on linguistics by John Lotz in *Frontiers of Knowledge in the Study of Man*, ed. by Lynn White, Jr., Harper, 1956. For a fuller survey read John B. Carroll, *The Study of Language*, Harvard University Press, 1953. Two standard treatments are Edward Sapir, *Language: An Introduction to the Study of Speech*, Harcourt, Brace, 1921, also available as a Harvest Book; and Leonard Bloomfield, *Language*, Holt, 1933. Larger contexts are suggested in *Language: An Enquiry into Its Meaning and Function*, ed. by Ruth Nanda Anshen, Harper, 1957.

3

What of classical literature, that mother of Western humanism? The formal commitment of scholarship to Greece and Rome remains what it has been—to understand the classical languages and keep this knowledge alive; to discover and maintain proper texts of classical authors; and to interpret these documents to the modern world. American scholarship came late into this field, and though its services have been useful (consider, for example, the work of the American Academy in Rome), though there are still Greek and Latin texts to be edited, though the recovery by archaeology of inscriptions from ruins and of papyri with their fragments of ancient texts creates a persisting task for the scholar, research is not likely to uncover another Aeschylus or Horace. Of course some great document in literature or politics may still turn up, but the revolution in this field has been a revolution of interpretation. The nineteenth century looked at the arts of Greece and Rome as ideal models, seeing them through the eyes of Johann Winckelmann and Goethe as timeless perfection. Symbolic were the plaster casts that used to adorn schoolrooms. The gods and goddesses all came out of Bulfinch's prettified *Age of Fable,* and episodes like Medea carving up her children and Oedipus tearing out his eyes were glossed over. The colorful, mercurial, and intelligent Greeks were metamorphosed into the staring marble statues many people still call "classical." The task of scholarship has therefore been to take the ancient world out of this Victorian Deepfreeze. Fresh interpretation has come about in the context of archaeological perspectives, the comparative method in religion and anthropology, modern psychology, and new knowledge about the connections of Greece and Rome with Asia Minor, Egypt, and the East. Moreover, the "new criticism" and a stricter sense of semantic meanings have aided this reinterpretation of the literary legacy in ways subtler and more profound than was possible to the generation of John P. Mahaffy. This "newness" is more apparent in the Greek field than in the Roman. It colors general works like H. D. F. Kitto's *The Greeks* (what Victorian would have dared to comment that the Athenians didn't have to push lawn mowers?) and V. Gordon Childe's *What Happened in History.* It also appears in the tone and values of recent translations of classical masterpieces by living scholar-poets such as Dudley Fitts, Richard Lattimore, and Rolfe Humphries. To compare Lattimore's translation of the *Agamemnon* with that by John Stuart Blackie in 1850 is to pass from the antimacassar to the automobile.

4

We find the Mediaeval Academy of America (founded 1925) ambitiously making the whole of medieval culture its topic, and in its journal, *Speculum,* holding the mirror up to a vast segment of life not at first glance of primary American interest.[9] We now realize what Gibbon did not fully realize, that the Byzantine Empire not only protected Europe for a thousand years, but also had a rich culture of its own, currently being studied at, among other places, Dumbarton Oaks in the District of Columbia.[10]

[9] Sanitation is not a customary subject of research, but few articles have done more to illustrate "the intimate discomforts, the household surprises and often the misplaced ingenuity of medieval life," says B. J. Whiting, than E. L. Sabine's articles in *Speculum,* "Butchering in London" (1933), "Latrines and Cesspools of Mediaeval London" (1934), and "City Cleaning in Mediaeval London" (1937).

[10] See in this connection the dynamic interpretation of Byzantine art in Malraux's *The Voices of Silence,* especially in the section on "The Metamorphoses of Apollo." Or read Steven Runciman, *Byzantine Civilization,* Longmans, Green, 1933, available in Meridian Books, 1956.

The twentieth century, it must not be forgotten, has produced Henry Adams's beautiful *Mont-Saint-Michel and
Chartres* (1913), the domestication of Neo-Scholasticism
in the United States, a definitive text of Chaucer's *Canter-
bury Tales* by Manly and Rickert (two scholars at the
University of Chicago), and extensive studies of Dante.[11]

The great instrument of literary (and linguistic) scholarship is the Modern Language Association of America,
which at its founding (1883) had a membership of forty
and now has a membership of over nine thousand. Its
quarterly magazine, *PMLA*,[12] has piled up over 70,000
pages in seventy-one volumes (1957); its books run from
Arthurian Legends in Mediaeval Art to its best seller (over
100,000 copies and still going strong), the *MLA Style
Sheet,* compiled by William Riley Parker in consultation
with eighty-one learned journals and thirty-three university presses; its interests comprise English, French, German, Spanish, Italian, Portuguese, Dutch, Swedish, the
Scandinavian languages, and so on; an early president was
James Russell Lowell; and its honorary members dot the
globe. We may compare the labors represented by these
thousands of articles and others like them to the nulli-
pores, who, bit by bit, build coral reefs into substan-
tiality.

We know immensely more about literary history now
than we knew in 1883. The obsession with evolution has
subsided ("The Evolution of the Novel" was once a favorite theme), and though scholars still struggle to establish

[11] See the remarkable article by Renato Poggioli, "Tragedy or Romance?
A Reading of the Paolo and Francesca Episode in Dante's *Inferno*,"
PMLA, LXXII (3): 313–358, June, 1957, in which, reading with fresh eyes
the famous but frayed episode of Paolo and Francesca in the Divine
Comedy, this scholar, examining the text word by word, puts the whole
episode into a new and human dimension. The tradition of Dante scholarship in America centers in Cambridge and counts among its famous
exponents Longfellow, Norton, and Grandgent.

[12] *Publication of the Modern Language Association of America.*

correct texts and expose forgeries,[13] the interests of literary scholars have been broadened to include living writers, American literature (not thought worth study in 1883), the history of ideas, the connections of literature and science, literature and society, literature and painting, and much else. Vast new sources of information have been made generally available in the publication of the papers and letters of personages like Thackeray, Dickens, Poe, Horace Walpole, Jefferson, Franklin, Jonathan Edwards, George Eliot, and James Boswell, to mention only work in English; and the modern foreign literatures have benefited from works as various as H. P. Thieme's bibliography of nineteenth-century French literature and the magisterial interpretation of Goethe by Karl Viëtor, self-exiled from Nazi Germany. American literary scholarship is respected and even envied in foreign lands today. Associated with scholarly work in literary history and interpretation and in some sense dependent on it—at any rate the connections between the two are vital—are the labors of the bibliographer. The twentieth century has seen the creation of the Bibliographical Society of America (1904), which, in addition to an immense amount of other work useful to booklovers, book collectors, librarians, and scholars, is issuing a ten-volume *Bibliography of American Literature* under the editorship of Jacob Blanck and financed by the Lilly Endowment of Indianapolis.

5

When we pass from the Atlantic community to knowledge of Asia, we note the activities of archaeologists, who, aided by biology and anthropology and busy in all parts of the

---

[13] *An Enquiry into the Nature of Certain Nineteenth Century Pamphlets* by John W. Carter and Graham Pollard, Scribner, 1934, is more exciting reading than most detective stories.

world, nevertheless most importantly altered the thinking
of Western man by forcing him to extend history backward from the traditional date of creation (4004 B.C.) until
today Christians accept without a shock chronological concepts like 40,000–20,000 B.C., the period of Neanderthal
culture. Concentrating first in Asia Minor, Greece, and
Egypt, archaeologists discovered, among other things, a
Babylonian flood story paralleling that in Genesis; and
more recently the dramatic story of the Dead Sea scrolls,
largely, though not wholly, deciphered by American scholarship, enriches our knowledge of Jewish culture during
the period of Jesus Christ. Biblical scholarship in the
United States has for decades associated itself with scholarship in other lands in the patient piecing together of impeccable texts of books of the Bible,[14] one of the influential results being the twentieth-century revised version of
that magnificent book.[15] Scholarly American interest in
Asia dates from the creation of the American Oriental

[14] Nothing is more remarkable than the ignorance in the United States,
which has among its creative founders the Bible commonwealths of New
England, concerning the achievements of modern Biblical scholarship.
Foreign scholarship looks with profound respect upon achievements like
Robert H. Pfeiffer's *Introduction to the Old Testament*, rev. ed., Harper,
1948, Walter E. Bundy's *Jesus and the First Three Gospels*, Harvard University Press, 1955, and the magisterial scholarship of Harry Austryn
Wolfson, whose *Philo* (Harvard University Press, first edition, 1947) and
The Philosophy of the Church Fathers, Volume I, *Faith, Trinity, Incarnation* (Harvard University Press, 1956) are among the intellectual triumphs
of our time.

[15] Inasmuch as the discovery of the Dead Sea scrolls is so recent that
scholarly opinion has not yet settled down, it is difficult to name a particular book for the general reader to consult. A readable translation, so
far as the originals have been deciphered, is *The Dead Sea Scriptures in
English Translation*, Doubleday, 1956. Although his interpretation has
been questioned, the account by J. M. Allegro, *The Dead Sea Scrolls*,
(Criterion, 1957) seems exciting. American readers will inevitably have an
inclination for Edmund Wilson, *The Scrolls from the Dead Sea*, Oxford
University Press, 1955. But literature on the subject is enormous, including excellent books by Krister Stendahl and Millar Burrows. Those interested in the cultural implications of other archaeological findings in
Asia Minor may care to consult Theodore H. Gaster, *The Oldest Stories
in the World*, Viking, 1952.

Society in 1842, but the farseeing program of its first president, John Pickering, is only now beginning to be fulfilled as the Association for Asian Studies[16] swings into action to aid its friendly rival in cultivating the vast field of study presented by modern Asia. Here as elsewhere humanistic scholarship draws upon the work of the social humanities.[17] Asian specialists are the first to admit that they have scarcely scratched the surface of their problems, however, and regret that popular interest in Asia has developed late. A pioneering interpretation like F. S. C. Northrop's *The Meeting of East and West* (1946) is significantly subtitled: *An Inquiry Concerning World Understanding,* and shows how much misunderstanding arises from the inability to agree about fundamental ideas east and west. Modest philosophic conferences in Hawaii, on the Pacific Coast, and elsewhere do what they can to decrease intellectual ignorance. But we are still children with respect to Asia. We are unfortunately cut off from the vast areas of China and Siberia by political differences that interfere with scholarly research. Nevertheless, it seems clear that the cultural development of Asia (however that vast area is defined) between the years 1100 and 1900, is likely to be of increasing interest to American scholarship. But it is now time to turn to the fine arts and to music.

6

None of the fine arts exhibits more remarkable changes than do music and painting in the twentieth century. The multiplication of art galleries and annual art exhibits in the United States, the number of "Sunday painters," and

[16] Formerly the Far Eastern Association.

[17] Suggestive in this connection is *An Appraisal of Anthropology Today,* ed. by Sol Tax *et al.,* University of Chicago Press, 1953. For the changed spirit in geography see the chapter by George H. T. Kimble on the topic in *Frontiers of Knowledge in the Study of Man.*

the increase in the availability and sale of excellent color reproductions of world masterpieces are paralleled only by the growth in number of American orchestras large and small, the vogue of chamber music, the serious interest in folk music and in popular music,[18] and, above all, the manufacture and sale of a vast library of excellent music ranging from entire operas to hillbilly records. Radio has, of course, been enormously influential. Though the living composer, like the living painter, can still complain of public obsession with conventional masterpieces, American painting and American musical life have attained a degree of stability only dreamed of by the generation of Edward MacDowell and Albert Pinkham Ryder. American musicologists have paralleled this interest in hearing and performing music, by extensive studies in the music of the world, and know more about the traditions of music in, say, Java or Africa than was known in 1900. Characteristic contributions are the *Columbia World Library of Folk and Primitive Music,* 17 vols. (records), 1951–57, edited by Alan Lomax, and Paul Henry Láng's *Music in Western Civilization* (1941). The American Musicological Society is the scholarly organization for research in music history. The College Art Association, composed of teachers, scholars, painters, museum directors, and curators, carries on parallel work in the fine arts. A statement by Rensselaer W. Lee of Princeton concerning the philosophy of this association, so excellently states the general theory of scholarship in the fine arts that with a slight change of wording it can serve for music as well:

The study of art in its relation to past civilizations enables us to understand how the different forms of art emerged from

---

[18] The Institute of Jazz at 108 Waverly Place, New York City, receives requests for information and recordings from all sorts and conditions of men, including enthusiasts from behind the Iron Curtain. See the article by Marshall W. Stearns in *Down Beat,* October 3, 1957.

different civilizations—why Greek, Gothic, Renaissance architecture, sculpture and painting took on the forms that they
did. Then we come to realize that the aesthetic forms of art
of the past are the expression of the fundamental values of
different ages and civilizations. And so the beauty of past
works of art, which the naive eye might cherish for itself and,
indeed, has every right to cherish, becomes for the historian
surcharged with meaning, the meaning given it by the point
of view of the age that produced it. This being true, art is a
teacher, not teaching narrowly, but very subtly and quietly.
The history of art reveals through the forms of architecture,
sculpture and painting the beliefs, ideals and aspirations, the
tastes of other epochs and thereby our experience is enriched
and an added dimension is given our knowledge and imagination. And we then see our own age in clearer perspective, and
understand and criticize it better in the light of what art has,
with particular vividness, revealed to us about the nature of
the past. And here the history of art, as one of the humanities
in a college or university education, joins hands not only with
history but with literature and philosophy. With them it extends our knowledge of man and nature, increases understanding and tolerance, and helps make us foolproof against those
mechanizing tendencies in the modern world which would
lead us to turn our faces away from the greatest creations of
the human spirit and deny the value of individual freedom
of expression.[19]

The work of the musicologist and the art historian is
buttressed by the work of the newly founded American
Society for Aesthetics (1942). American enterprise in this
area is exemplified in the *Journal of Aesthetics and Art
Criticism* published by the society, and by Thomas
Munro's *Toward Science in Aesthetics* (1956). In 1956

[19] See in this connection "A Statement on the Place of the History of
Art in the Liberal Arts Curriculum; by a Committee of the College Art
Association of America"; and "A Statement on the Practice of Art Courses;
by a Committee of the College Art Association of America," both published in the mid-forties.

this society led in organizing the Third International Congress on Aesthetics, held in Venice.[20]

7

We cannot in this rich field examine everything. We have noted that the extraordinary labors of archaeologists here[21] and abroad have added such vast areas of time and space to the past of mankind as almost to embarrass historians. The excellent work of the American Numismatic Society includes sustaining a fine museum in New York, not as well known to the public as it should be.[22] We can only touch on the labors of the American Folklore Society[23]

[20] Concerning this general approach to the historico-cultural problem a distinguished historian, after reading this manuscript, writes: "I have a pet theory about the history of art and science, too. If the world lasts long enough, my guess is that gradually the major questions historians will put to their documents will not deal with politics and economics, and major philosophies of history will not be variant versions of economic or political determinism; rather, such questions and philosophies will turn on the conditions (including economic and political conditions) that made possible the great achievements of man in art, science, etc. Historians will then be inclined (perhaps too much inclined, but I would gladly run the risk) to make politics and economics subordinate to the understanding of the world's cultures."

[21] With us the formal professional body is the Archaeological Institute of America, largely the creation of Charles Eliot Norton in 1879. It began its diggings at the site of the Greek city of Assos in Asia Minor, later instituted excavations in both the New World and elsewhere in the Old, and has since been active in discussion, publication, and popular education. It publishes a popular quarterly, *Archaeology*, and sponsors educational films on Greece, Egypt, and other key areas. Its professional magazine is the *American Journal of Archaeology*.

[22] The museum is at Broadway and 156th Street. The *Numismatic Notes and Monographs* of the society now total 137 volumes, covering subjects as diverse as "Early Chinese Coinage," "Counterfeiting in Colonial New York," and "Temples of Rome as Coin Types." Since 1952 it has maintained an annual graduate seminar in numismatics, believed to be unique. In 1958 it celebrated its centenary.

[23] Folklore is more than collecting children's play and party games. It throws light on primitive psychology in one direction and in another furnishes material for art and literature. Consider, for example, the various books and poems that have been built on legends of Tony Beaver, Mike Fink, and Paul Bunyan, or such a stage success as Marc Connelly's

and those of the History of Science Society, fields in which scholarship is alert and vigorous. The "social humanities" deserve more attention than can here be given them, since scholarship in the social sciences is complementary, not antagonistic, to humanistic scholarship, and our knowledge of human nature has been vastly increased by the work of anthropologists,[24] economists, sociologists, political scientists, social psychologists, geographers, and legal theorists.[25]

Green Pastures. Its musical influence includes Dvorak's *New World Symphony* and the successes of such serious ballad singers as Burl Ives. Tom Lehrer's parodies of folk songs show another direction of influence.

[24] This is as good an opportunity as any to summarize Dr. Loren C. Eiseley's cogent and amusing notation of change in thought brought about by anthropology. "I quote," he says, "from *The Testimony of the Rocks,* a group of essays composed in the 1850's by Hugh Miller, a mid-nineteenth-century British geologist. Miller speaks as follows: 'Let me remark that the further we remove from the original center of the race [Mt. Ararat?], the more degraded and sunk do we find the several varieties of humanity. In the backwoods of America, in southern Africa, in Australia, and in the Polynesian islands, the whole Adamic type has been asserting its superiority and annihilating before it the degraded . . . the further we remove in any direction from the Adamic center, the more animalized and sunk do we find the various tribes or races. Wherever man . . . has fallen least, whatever he has retained at least intellectually [of] the Divine Image, this Caucasian type of feature and figure, with, of course, certain national modifications he also retains.'" Dr. Eiseley then summarizes Miller's pejorative descriptions of Lapps, Negroes, Mongolians, and Fuegians, all "lapses from an original Caucasian type" in Miller's opinion, and quotes that savant as follows: "They do not represent, save in hideous caricature, the glorious creature molded of old by the hand of the Divine Worker."

Here, says Dr. Eiseley, we have "a perfect exemplification of the doctrine of the Fall applied to the solution of the racial problem. It contains all the naive ethnocentrism and assured pride of position that so often accompany imperial growth . . . the shift in the use made of the age-area concept within a few decades of Miller's interpretation . . . is a profound tribute to man's capacity for growth. Today, Father Teilhard and other scholars among us seek the 'Adamic center' in the shape of crude but rising small-brained bipeds whose ancestral trail runs directly to some clump of trees on the edge of the East African savannah. . . . This great act of self-abnegation, hidden among yellowing scientific documents, remains, in my belief, man's most remarkable feat of pure intellect to date." *An Appraisal of Anthropology Today,* p. 22. "Father Teilhard" is Pierre Teilhard de Chardin.

[25] In setting up three panels of experts to discuss the philosophic concept of individualism East and West, the American Council of Learned

But what, in conclusion, can be said of those all-embracing topics, central to humanistic scholarship, history and philosophy?

8

It is by now evident that humanistic scholarship and humane learning live and operate both in the context of history and in the context of philosophy. History is itself a form of philosophic evaluation, and the history of philosophy part of the knowledge of philosophy. Each humanistic discipline partakes of philosophical value and of historical method and point of view. The problem is now to narrow the camera lens to history and philosophy in a more professional sense of these terms.

History in the conventional sense of the scholarly interpretation of public events and of the motives of human beings concerned in them has produced so vast a harvest of print in the twentieth century that the mind staggers at the intellectual energy displayed, even if one confines oneself only to history written in English. So far as larger works are concerned, building on examples from the nineteenth century, history has characteristically gone in for co-operative, many-volumed enterprises, each book (or chapter) written by a specialist, the whole supervised by a central board. Typical are the *Cambridge Modern History*, currently being revised, *The American Nation: A History* series, now being replaced, and *The History of American Life* series. Fullness and accuracy are obvious virtues of such undertakings; unevenness of style and tone, and uncertainty of a central point of view, are inevitable defects. Single volumes by historians tend to be monographs,

Societies in 1957 as a matter of course included historians of law, economists, political scientists, and sociologists among their experts, in addition to philosophers, linguists, and historians.

treatises, or biographies,[26] and the writing of textbooks is a major professional occupation in America. For better or worse the influence of the textbook publisher is evident in this genre. The subject matter of historical writing is still in the main Europe and North America. Latin America, Asia, and Africa as subjects are still in arrears.

Although the annual addresses of successive presidents of the American Historical Association commonly discuss the theory of history, no clear picture emerges from them. The twentieth century has seen the rise and decline of economic determinism as a decisive formula in historical change, it has witnessed a decline in political history and an increase in institutional and social history, it presently sees a rise in military history and various experimentations in the history of ideas (intellectual history), religious history, regional history, and cultural history. Stir and dissatisfaction may reasonably be glossed as evidence of growth. In some sense scholarship for the last fifty years has been more interested in destroying fallacies and questioning generalizations than was the nineteenth century, a period overly given to discovering "law" in historical processes. It is at least possible that some future Gibbon or Leopold von Ranke will find the information at his command far more accurate, and the tools with which to work far more refined, than were either in 1900.

It is, moreover, unfair to say that modern historical scholarship has produced no work of epic dimension. Oswald Spengler's abstruse but powerful *Decline of the West* (1918, 1922) brought back into prominence the metaphysics of historical change, and H. G. Wells's *Outline of History* (1920), persuasive and popular, with its running accompaniment of dissenting footnotes by specialists, is still read. One is tempted to include Vilfredo

[26] A return to the many-volumed Victorian biography is evident in such books as Douglas Southall Freeman's life of Robert E. Lee.

Pareto's four volumes (in translation), *The Mind and Society* (1935), under this rubric, since Pareto's theme, like that of Herbert Spencer, is the dynamism of historic development. But just as one thought the providential theory of history had disappeared, Arnold J. Toynbee published in ten volumes *A Study of History* (1934–1954). Toynbee not only sees the hand of God in the rise and fall of civilizations, but he imputes a Christian sense of sin to the process. To him as to Gibbon, as he tells us in his tenth volume, illumination was vouchsafed. Gazing during a long May day and evening at the site of ancient and modern Sparta, he was eventually "convicted of a horrifying sense of the sin manifest in the conduct of human affairs," and, brooding over catastrophe, "the impact of the Laconian landscape on his classical *Weltanschauung* . . . impressed on his mind two lasting lessons—one concerning the historical geography of Continental European Greece and the other concerning the morphology of the history of civilization." [27] Toynbee's theological interpretation has by no means won universal acceptance.

But if specialists are understandably reluctant to accept the sweeping theory that history displays the judgments of a Christian God, Toynbee has an uncomfortable habit of asking philosophic questions which, despite his appeal to the examples of writers varying from Josephus to James Ford Rhodes, history has not yet gathered the strength to answer:

This *fin-de-siècle* liberal Western hope had been a secularized version of Christ's promise in the Gospels: 'Verily I say unto

---

[27] *A Study of History*, Oxford University Press, X, pp. 107–110. He records a series of other mystical moments, *op. cit.*, pp. 130–140. The section entitled "Poetry in the Facts of History" is in fact a series of Christianized moral judgments (pp. 113–125), and "The Quest for a Meaning Behind the Facts of History" culminates (pp. 143–144) in a vast expansion, so to speak, of Pope's "Universal Prayer" but with ritualistic overtones foreign to the eighteenth century.

you that there be some of them that stand here which shall not taste of death till they have seen the Kingdom of God come with power.' How was it that this hapless generation had lived to see, instead, not the second coming of the Son of Man, but the advent of Antichrist? What fell miscarriage had over-taken the world-wide and perpetual peace that had been con-fidently augured in A.D. 1851 at the opening of a Great Exhibi-tion in London and had then apparently been achieved twenty years later, after the end of the Franco-Prussian War of A.D. 1870–1871? How had this peace come to be shattered in A.D. 1914 and A.D. 1939 by the successive explosions of two world wars in one lifetime? How had the twentieth century of the Christian Era come to see the eighteenth century's "laws of civilized warfare" thrown to the winds? How had Human Nature prevailed upon itself to perpetrate the atrocities which Turkish hands had committed against the Armenians, and German hands against the Belgians, the Jews, the Poles, and all their other victims? . . . How, through this welter of war and crime, had the political map of the *Oikoumene* come to be changed beyond all recognition? . . . How had the number of the Great Powers in a Western World come to be reduced, within a period of thirty-two years, from the figure of eight at which it had stood at the outbreak of a First World War in A.D. 1914 to the figure of two at which it stood at the close of a Second World War in A.D. 1945? How was it that these two survivors, the Soviet Union and the United States, were both of them, located outside Western Europe? [28]

Such, in the opinion of the most prominent historian in the English-speaking world, are some of the tragic but exciting problems confronting historical research today.

9

If the field of history is enormous, that of philosophy is diffuse. Santha Rau is presumably justified in saying that

[28] *Op. cit.,* pp. 91–92.

philosophy is more generally honored in India than it is
in the United States, since according to her every Indian
village has its philosopher. Repressing a mischievous desire to comment on the village philosopher in the United
States, one must keep carefully in mind the distinction
between general wisdom and the technical work of trained
philosophers going about professional tasks paralleling
those of the economist or the mathematician. Our present
interest is in philosophers in this professional sense. The
century opened in the Golden Age of American philosophy when Josiah Royce, William James, George Santayana,
and John Dewey were each propounding systematic
thought in his own way. In this brilliant quartet philosophy in America reached a height it has not yet regained.
Despite admirable thinkers now living, it seems fair to
say that no systematic philosophy propounded by any
American since the death of Dewey seems likely to exercise
the influence of the thinkers of the Golden Age.

But philosophers have not been idle. A basic task in
philosophy is the critical examination of two allied problems: how can we know anything in *any* field of thought,
and how can we trust that knowledge? Stunning advances
in mathematical and physical theories leading to the Einsteinian intellectual revolution of our time have given
philosophy so much to analyze that it is not surprising that
no general system now dominates the field. Under the
merciless knife of intellectual analysis—the current preoccupation in philosophy in English, almost of necessity—
every system of idealism has been found to be inconsistent
or somewhere fallacious. If the nature of the metaphysical
problem at the moment puzzles the layman, he may at least
note the fascination of symbolic logic. Enthusiastic proponents regard it as a new way to advance learning. Because the present temper of American philosophy is thus
analytical, that sort of synthesis out of which systems de-

velop is not at the moment much in evidence. But an enormous refinement of analytical method—a sharpening of the tools like that in history—is apparent on every hand.

The matter is of more than passing importance for the humanities. In contrast to the scientist with his opportunity for a place in industry, and to the social scientist with his chance at jobs in government or business, the humanistic scholar is in the main confined to the academic world. But there are grades of opportunity even among humanists—scholars in history and literature, for example, having occasional job opportunities in libraries and special institutes, scholars in art sometimes training for museum work, and so on. The occupational area of philosophers, however, is in the academic world, since government does not employ metaphysicians, and business and industry do not hire logicians as they hire chemists. The commitment of philosophy since the days of Plato and earlier has been a commitment to teaching; and it is therefore of moment to note the appearance in 1945 of a volume sponsored by the American Philosophical Association and written by five philosophers, entitled *Philosophy in American Education*. The substance of the book was distilled from meetings held at strategic points in the United States and from communications sent to the committee from interested Americans. A central chapter, "Aspects of the Role of Philosophy in Civilization," by Charles W. Hendel of the committee, is pertinent. If the volume be thought of as setting goals in philosophy, development must be in the direction of gearing philosophy with democratic culture, as this paragraph makes clear:

Whence is to come the public *understanding* of . . . principles basic to our society? . . . Our civilization is on a democratic basis, not simply because of certain philosophical ideals but because of the whole drift and tendency of history. There is now a democratic responsibility vested in all the people. How are they to learn what they need to know for the exercise of their political rights and duties? Are they to get tutoring merely from politicians who can talk a disarming patter about freedom and make a noble word stale and cheap by invoking it in connection with every measure and on every occasion? Or are they to derive their notions from the publicity advertising of interested parties in our economy who advance their enterprising postwar plans for getting ahead of everybody else in the world under the name of an equal freedom for all peoples to compete, and who really confuse two entirely opposite motives of social policy, the motive of domination and that of liberty and justice? Or are the people to learn the clear, essential truth only in the disinterested teachings of philosophers who are clean out of all politics and business? It is not so simple as that . . . our business is to understand *our own civilization* and not simply to take over and teach already formulated "liberal" ideas. . . . A review of past experience shows us . . . that philosophy is significant when it works in a generous partnership.[29]

If the partnership of philosophy at the moment, generous or not, is with science in the philosophic endeavor to ascertain the basis of the dependability both of knowledge and of the intellectual process, the partnership is not irrevocable,[30] and there is some reason to suppose there is a slow swing back to the Platonic goal of the philosopher as citizen and as magistrate implicit in the paragraph quoted. *Philosophy in American Education* is now twelve or thirteen years behind us, and the philosophic problem of sustaining and explicating democracy has become more rather than less cogent as Russia and the United States confront each other across both outer space and the spaces of this world. No American philosopher during the period has

[29] Brand Blanshard *et al., Philosophy in American Education: Its Tasks and Opportunities,* Harper, 1945, pp. 185–187.
[30] See in this connection C. E. M. Joad, *A Critique of Logical Positivism,* University of Chicago Press, 1950.

advocated fascism, despotism, tyranny, or any other form of political absolutism. There is, apparently, no American equivalent of either Hobbes or Machiavelli. If present developments in metaphysical thinking may be vaguely described as tool sharpening, the tools so sharpened are not going to be employed against the democratic ideal of the state.

EIGHT

Scholarship, Art, Criticism

This report has failed of its purpose if its reader still
believes that humane learning dwells in an ivory tower
that has no opening on the world. The whole drift of
what we have been saying is to insist upon the organic
connection between the rich life of the humanities and
the vitality of American culture. It may, then, seem inconsistent now to turn to the relation of humane learning
to contemporary art and criticism. But this issue needs
clarification. Charges of uselessness, lack of sympathy,
irrelevance, massive wrongheadedness, and even hostility
are made against learning by artists, teachers, newspaper-
men, educational administrators, business publicists, and
others; and it is to an examination of these complaints that
we come.

The quarrel concerns the relation of humane learning
to certain broad, yet definable, American interests: contemporary art (or, more loosely, "creative activity"), certain aspects of criticism, the demand for "value judgments"
from the humanities, and, finally, the nature of humane
teaching. This chapter will look into the problem of creativity and of criticism; its successors will discuss the puzzle
of "value judgments" and some responsibilities involved in
teaching the humanities.

Even at the risk of oversimplification it will make for

clarity if we put the problem of humane learning and creative activity in its extreme form. Briefly, the theory runs, every human being is creative—capable, that is, of a unique outlook on life comparable to that of an artist; and therefore the primary duty of education is to release this energy by encouraging the individual to express himself in whatever activity, often one of the arts, seems most congenial to him. Some persons are by nature and nurture more likely to become professional artists than are others, and, in such cases particularly, to impede or crush talent beneath a load of historicity is to sin against the holy ghost. But even though a student manifests a lesser degree of creative ability, he can be led to an "appreciation" of the arts, or some one of them, by proper teaching. Proper teaching in this context means direct exposure to works of art, without the elaborate apparatus of scholarship; and this exposure, so the argument runs, is best conducted by a sympathetic teacher rather than by a learned man.

Negatively it is argued that the teaching of literature (or, rather, of literary history and "philology"), art history, musicology, or any other branch of humane learning deflects, undervalues, or in practice kills this desirable mode of self-development ("self-expression"). Since "we are all artists," those who fail to develop their creativity or their appreciation fail, not because of lack of some degree of talent in this direction, but because of the lifeless quality of learning. The scholar, absorbed in contemplating and analyzing the masterpieces of past time, becomes in this view a kind of enemy. In the first place, he is unsympathetic to contemporary art for two reasons. He does not "live" in the contemporary world and is, therefore, unable to understand the expression of its life. Since he cannot know whether recent productions are masterpieces or not, he declines to interest himself in what, from his standpoint, is inferior and ephemeral. In the second place, since nothing pleases him but what is attested, he crushes young students under the weight of perfection and tradition—a perfection they cannot possibly attain, a tradition that is meaningless because irrelevant to present problems. Partly on the analogy of laboratory science, partly because schools of art, conservatories of music, courses in "creative writing," and summer writers' conferences concentrate upon the production of art, with only minimal reference to the masterpieces of the past, it is, finally, assumed that the sole purpose of teaching art is to develop creative or performing ability.[1]

There is force in the argument, so much, indeed, that colleges and universities which in 1900 would not have dreamed of such appointments now commonly have a musician, practicing painter, poet, dramatist, writer of fiction, or critic "in residence," or maintain a string quartet, or otherwise serve as patrons of art. As a group such institutions offer a vast variety of instruction in creative activity, whether it be courses in composition, teaching the ballet, a curriculum in the arts of design, active work in the theater, instruction in musical composition and performance, or programs in radio and television work. Some universities maintain annual lectureships filled by artists and critics, of which the Charles Eliot Norton professorship at Harvard is typical. Others sustain theaters producing original, "classic," and "Broadway" plays on virtually a professional basis. Ebullient undergraduate life, moreover, commonly includes a band, an orchestra, stu-

---

[1] There is, however, one important difference between music and the other arts in this context. The young composer cannot go to work until he has mastered the theory of harmony, the principles of orchestration, and other technical matters, products of traditional practice and learning, whereas the young painter need not know anything about anatomy or perspective, and the young writer is not expected to be familiar with traditional theories of style, aesthetics, or other elements of the grammar of his art.

dent writing clubs, student singing societies and light opera companies, a student newspaper, a yearbook, and, more sporadically, a "serious" literary magazine, and so forth. Inasmuch as members of the faculty are in one capacity or another involved with these enterprises, the notion of implacable antagonism between humanistic scholars and the creative arts requires some modification.

2

Nevertheless, the problem is not thus easily disposed of. The argument cuts deeper than the existence of a painter in residence or than undergraduate activities on the campus. It rests, in fact, upon at least three fundamental notions. One is the assumption, going back to the romantic movement, that original genius is by definition inspired, unpredictable, essentially unteachable, and always novel. Genius becomes genius in revolt; and therefore any major attempt to discipline it in the schools is an effort to subdue it. The second assumption is characteristically in the American vein. Emerson wrote that we have listened too long to the courtly muses of Europe. The resulting imitativeness long confined art in America to an inferior and parochial status. Thus it became, and is still, our duty to produce something unique, unparalleled, essentially American, democratic, popular, or of the New World—the phrase varies. Finally—the third idea—there is nothing in the history of mankind to parallel the appalling troubles of our age—the time of Freud, Lenin, Hitler, Gandhi, Einstein; of frightful wars, insoluble economic, sociological, and political problems; of loss of belief, loss of faith, loss of honor, loss of security; of the intercontinental ballistic missile, the hydrogen bomb, artificial satellites, and impending explorations of outer space. Therefore it is useless for moderns to seek comfort or wisdom in the thought and art of ages now long dead, ages which, though they thought they had their burdens, confronted no such tragic agony as is ours. The masterpieces that can speak to us are few—Goya, Kierkegaard, the enigmatic *Don Giovanni* of Mozart, Dürer's "Melancholia," the philosophical relativism of Ludwig Wittgenstein and Rudolf Carnap. Do not, then, weaken our struggle with despair by calling our attention away to remote problems of other times.[2]

These arguments have varying weight. The third would seem to be self-defeating, since, granted that the atomic age is the age of anxiety, the solution of its problems would seem to require more wisdom rather than less, and to rule out all the past experience of man on this planet needlessly cripples present-day artists and thinkers, who, whatever the theory, do not in fact behave as the theory requires. Two examples from among many must illustrate this truth: when James Joyce wants to explicate the psychological tangles that form our dark night of the soul, he models his *Ulysses* upon the Odyssey of Homer, wherein, at long last but nonetheless surely, Odysseus comes to his own hearthstone; and when Igor Stravinsky wants movingly to present the predicament of modern man lost and baffled in a cruel and careless universe, he writes his oratorio-opera *Oedipus Rex*, seeking in music the selfsame peace his great predecessor Sophocles found in drama. But to understand Homer and Sophocles requires, precisely, the aid of humane learning.

The second argument has more weight. During earlier decades the weakness of the arts in America was, indeed, imitativeness. They were academic in the wrong sense. A Washington Allston was smothered by the Venetians, to whom he yielded allegiance; a Longfellow, remarkable technician that he was, imitated all the lights and shades

[2] But see in this connection Charles Frankel, *The Case for Modern Man,* Harper, 1956.

of European romanticism; a MacDowell, finding small stimulus in "native" Indian music, lost himself in Brahmsian musical rhetoric. There are many other like instances. Unfortunately for logic other examples prove the contrary: Jefferson, steeped in the European Enlightenment, was nevertheless a founder of our culture; Cooper, awkward imitator of Scotch and English fiction, created Leatherstocking the unique; Poe, immensely (if superficially) well read, was an original genius; and Lincoln, shaped by the Bible, Shakespeare, Bunyan, Defoe, and Robert Burns, yet seems to us to have sprung from the fresh soil of the unexhausted West. Possibly more depends upon individual endowment and less upon training than the theory allows for.

Finally, there is the matter of creative originality. Certainly it is commonplace to find any rising generation of artists in rebellion against the practice of their elders—the Pre-Raphaelites denouncing the academies and "Sir Sloshua," the writers of our 1920's turning furiously against the genteel tradition, especially as it was taught in the colleges, twentieth-century composers striking savagely at the long domination of orchestral music by Wagner, and so on. But it may be asked whether creative genius and creative epochs are as unrelated to the past as the theory stipulates. Of course creative artists are not alike, and of course those who deny the relevance of any history will see no relevance in other creative periods. Nevertheless, if the prophecy prove true that we are living in a great age of the arts in America, there is some relevance in asking how other great creative ages came into being.

Upon examination it would appear that most great periods in Western culture have had their beginnings in rediscovery. Thus the Augustan age in Rome came about through a generous desire to emulate the arts of Greece, and the Carolingian Renaissance of the early Middle Ages was the product of a renewed and lively interest in Latin literature. The European Renaissance, wonderful epoch that it was, was set in motion by the rediscovery and reinterpretation of antiquity, creating opera in an effort to rival Greek tragedy, producing historians after the manner of the ancients, building architectural masterpieces after designs descending from imperial Rome, and expressing in tragedy and epic that sense of the nobler possibilities of humanity men like Shakespeare and Milton discovered in the past. The Age of Reason—the period of Descartes, Newton, Molière, Racine, Pope, Diderot, Lessing, Fielding, Dr. Johnson, Franklin, Burke, Gibbon, Jefferson—found its incentive in the classic geometry of Euclid, the classic aesthetics of Aristotle and Longinus, and the classic morality of the ancients. By and by the vast and variegated romantic movement fed upon the arts of the Middle Ages, the "Gothick" North, the music of Scotland, Ireland, Hungary, Spain, Oriental tales, new and intensely human versions of Greek myth and Roman story, legends of the Aztecs and the Incas, and much more. If the present age truly turned a blind eye to the past, it would be peculiar in doing so. But of course it does no such thing.

Even the legend that genius is forever rebellious is open to correction. Commonly genius begins by imitating an older artist. Beethoven goes to school to Haydn, young Milton steeps himself in "metaphysical" verse, a Western painter like the modern C. S. Price learns draftsmanship from the more conventional Charles Russell, Manet reworks Goya in "The Execution of Maximilian" and "Olympia," and Richard Strauss has to rid himself of Wagnerism in the *Guntram* of 1894. Even a William Blake is not, so to speak, revolutionary from the egg; though he never went to school and therefore could not suffer from the oppression of the learned, his *Poetical Sketches,* wonderful as they are, owe something to the Elizabethans, something to seventeenth-century lyricists, something to Ossian, and something to the fashionable verse of the late eighteenth century; and the source of the pure line in his amazing drawings has been found, among other places, in the Gothic style he picked up from drawing copies of monuments in Westminster Abbey. The doctrine that humane learning of past time is a kind of pedantry imposed upon genius from without does not seem to be in accord with fact.

Indeed, if one defines pedantry as the lifeless imitation of models, coupled with the exaltation of minutiae and faith in a dogma of correctness outside of which there is no salvation, the charge of pedantry, amusingly enough, should be rather lodged against the teachers of creativity. Who that has visited three or four annual exhibitions of contemporary painting but must lament the imitativeness of the canvases displayed? These painters have not looked at objects reflecting or absorbing light in an Einsteinian universe so much as they have looked at Jack Levine, Yasuo Kuniyoshi, or Marc Chagall, or at Robert Motherwell, Franz Kline, Jackson Pollock, Hans Hoffmann, Mark Tobey, or some other god of modern idolatry. Courses in "criticism" commonly apply a few dogmatic formulas about myth, rhetoric, symbol, and layers of meaning to authors who are eternally the same—James, Hawthorne, Melville, Kafka, and so on. Courses in "poetry" concentrate upon T. S. Eliot, William Carlos Williams, Wallace Stevens, Marianne Moore, William Butler Yeats, and others; courses in "creative writing" turn out their juvenile imitations of Hemingway, Tennessee Williams, Graham Greene, or some other popular author. How hard it is to distinguish the work of one young musician from that of another, although the trained ear catches echoes of

Hindemith, Ives, Vaughn Williams, Stravinsky, and so on!
Youth imitates. Nothing is more conventional than revolt.
It is not humane learning that creates this monotony, this
timidity, this regimentation of the soul. "When people
are free to do as they please," says Eric Hoffer, "they usually imitate each other. Originality is deliberate and
forced, and partakes of the nature of a protest. A society
which gives unlimited freedom to the individual, more
often than not attains a disconcerting sameness . . . when
imitation runs its course in a wholly free society it results
in a uniformity which is not unlike a mild tyranny." [3]

The use of humane learning in the context of creativity
is that it urges the artist to break with this tyranny, to discover the suggestiveness in other cultures, other masterpieces than the present worship of a few stereotype models.
Falstaff, Micawber, Don Quixote, Emma Bovary, Criseyde,
Paolo and Francesca were created before Freud, T. S.
Eliot, and Toynbee; the immense world of painting, architecture, sculpture, mosaics, decoration patiently offers a
thousand hints about ways of seeing the world over and
beyond the insight of Dali or of Picasso; the cosmic visions
of St. Augustine, Lucretius, Dante, Virgil, the Norse sagas,
Confucius, Shelley, Marcus Aurelius Antoninus are ever
present to correct, or strengthen, or enrich our own; and
this infinite variety, this vast treasure house of art and
theory, philosophy and personality is freely available to
us as it has been to others for years, continually adding to
its contents, moreover, every form of beauty and delight.
Of course there are pedants behind the lectern of the classroom just as there are pedants in the studio and the re-
hearsal chamber, but the point is that all virtue does not
lie with contemporaneity solely, nor all dullness with the

[3] *The Passionate State of Mind and Other Aphorisms*, Harper, 1955, p.
21.

organized knowledge we call learning. But let Bernard
Berensen speak:

You can cast off each separate masterpiece created by the arts
in recent generations or the whole of the sixty-odd centuries
during which art, as distinct from artifacts, was being created.
You can perhaps succeed in ridding yourself of all remembered concepts, facts, ideas, of the recent as well as of the
remote past. You can throw overboard every mental heritage
that consciousness has prized. When you have done so, where
are you? What has become of you? You remain incapable of
uttering a word that has not its roots buried deep in the remotest past. You cannot open your lips without being used as
a mouthpiece by myriads upon myriads of the dead. You are
but little more than a disk recording the reproducing traditions that no awareness can fathom, traditions deposited during countless thousands of years in your anatomical and
physiological structure, in your tissues, in your nervous and
glandular systems. Yet you fancy that you are free to start
afresh as men did hundreds of millenniums ago. In that remote age he had to fight only against other wild beasts, and
the figments of his own brain. Now he must walk the tread-
mill of mechanical forces that he himself has constructed but
from which, now that they dominate him, he cannot wrench
himself free. He may yet live to regret the ease with which
he threw away the conscious traditions that were operative in
humanizing him. He may come to sigh for what it was to have
been an American, an Englishman, an Italian, a Frenchman,
a German in the years when our civilization seemed so secure,
and its foundations dug so deep into the past, that we could
not imagine their being shaken.[4]

In the search for stability, if the foundations of a dwelling
place are shaken, nothing is gained by moving into a tepee.

[4] *Aesthetics and History,* Pantheon Books, 1948; Anchor Books, 1954, pp.
270–271.

3

This discussion has up to now principally confined itself to "creativity." But the problem of criticism remains, a problem in one sense simpler, in another sense more complicated than the question of the relation of humane learning to creativity. If one assumes with Matthew Arnold that the aim of criticism is to learn and propagate the best that is known or thought in the world, or if one holds with Walter Pater that every intellectual product must be judged from the point of view of the age and of the people in which it was produced, because perfection is to be found in many styles and forms, then the aim of criticism is virtually identical with the ideal of humane learning. Or if one holds that the educated critic should possess himself of all doctrines of art relevant to a phase of art or a work of art he is examining, then, too, the ideal critic does not differ from the ideal man of learning. Or if one assumes that the aim of criticism is the formation of taste either by creating that positive sense of enjoyment William Hazlitt calls gusto or by creating that sense of discrimination Arnold has in mind when he characterizes culture as the study of perfection, there is no disharmony between the aim of learning and the purpose of criticism. Clearly the purposes of learning are to learn and propagate the best, to understand artifact and document in the light of the conditions that brought them forth, to examine and judge systems of philosophy, including aesthetic theories, and, by enriching individual taste, to increase and refine pleasure. Indeed, the great traditional critics have also been humanists, as witness Aristotle, Schiller, the Schlegels, Lessing, Sainte-Beuve, Brandes, Diderot, Herder, Coleridge, and Arnold; or Vasari, Berlioz, Tovey, Sir Joshua Reynolds, Burkhardt, Winckelmann, Schumann, Busoni, and Berenson in arts other than literature. So far there is no real problem.

Under the influence of evolutionary theory, however, humanistic scholarship, particularly in language and literature, during the last decades of the nineteenth century and the opening years of the twentieth, went in heavily for the genetic study of art. Not only was a literary type supposed to "evolve," but the explanation of a work of art—say, a comedy by Shakespeare—was sought less in the work itself than in the circumstances surrounding its production, such as events in the writer's life, the sources of his materials, the influence of conventions upon his work, and the cultural and social environment in which it first appeared. It became at times, or so it seemed, less important to read *Macbeth* for its pity and terror than to find out what relation the drama had to the succession of James VI of Scotland to the throne of England. Precisely as scholarly editions of Latin text often contain more annotation to the page than they do lines of the original work, so, it appeared to many, humanistic scholarship was leading away from the work rather than into it. An investigation reported by I. A. Richards (*Practical Criticism*, 1929) revealed that readers, even readers in the academic world, were in fact unable to read a poem or to agree upon its meaning. Erudition did not help them. This discovery came in a period when philosophers, particularly British philosophers, were heavily engaged in analyzing language as a mode of communication (*The Meaning of Meaning*, 1936, by C. K. Ogden and I. A. Richards was in part the product of this movement), and this new movement in criticism paralleled the work of the logical positivists in concentrating their attention upon the analysis of language.

In extreme form the new critical movement seemed to deny the validity of historical erudition as a mode of understanding a literary work. The meaning of a literary work, they argued, lies within the work, not in the surrounding biographical and historical data. Quintessentially, the meaning of any work is to be found in the moral integrity of the artist's professional vision, not in any didactic gloss or impulse. The creative act is in truth as serious a human activity as any other human activity. It is to be judged in its own light and its own right. Therefore, the critic, so ran the theory, must repudiate, or at the least subordinate, all information "outside" the work to the central problem of the work itself.

Exploring the psychology of the creative act inevitably then led critics, themselves influenced by the climate of opinion of their time, in the direction of irrational or depth psychology; and, interpreting the text of a given work, they sometimes discovered or imputed to it systems or expressions of myth, symbolism, and covert meaning presumably arising out of the author's unconscious but not invariably evident in the plain text of the work. Tensions were inevitably created between scholarship and criticism. Moreover, the doctrine that the meaning of a work is in the work itself, and not outside it, spread to arts other than literature. Thus, a contemporary painter, asked what his canvas "means," is likely to respond: "Well, there it is. It says what it means." The implication for the unenlightened is that if they do not, after sufficient contemplation, discover meaning, it is just too bad.

Reform succeeds by excess; but it seems clear in 1958 that the warfare between critic and scholar was something of a sham battle. The critic has done an immense amount of good in reminding the scholar that humane learning, to be humane, must forever make the work of art central in any problem about art.[5] That repudiating learning can

---

[5] But it is obviously legitimate to scan a work of art for other purposes than aesthetic satisfaction. Thus the Homeric poems are properly not

ever be quite so total as the extreme form of this critical theory implies may be at once denied. In the first place, so far as literature is concerned and to some degree the other arts, the critic must deal with the language in which the work is shaped, but competently to understand words, phrases, constructions, figures of speech and allusions, he must have immediate recourse to historical scholarship, even if he do no more than look up words in a dictionary. So in painting. The meaning of a canvas does not necessarily lie in its immediate manifestation. A naïve "modern" wandering through a museum and coming upon a painting rather hieratic in character representing a tall female figure carrying her eyes on a platter or a leaf, may, indeed correctly date the picture as fifteenth-century, yet incorrectly infer that the surrealism of Dali or Chirico has been anticipated by five hundred years. The fact is, however, that the painter had no notions whatsoever about surrealism; all he was doing was giving his concept of St. Lucy, who as a martyr had her eyes torn out. He followed a standard system of iconography of his time. The beauty of Shakespeare's sonnets is no way increased by an attempt to answer the question: "Who was W.H.?" It is, however, virtually impossible to make even simple sense out of a good many passages in poems by T. S. Eliot, Ezra Pound, and other favorites among the moderns unless one reads them, so to speak, in the midst of a large reference library. The great virtue of the critical movement under discussion is that it encouraged slow and careful study of appropriate texts; its great weakness is that it has lost the allegiance of general readers, who find that its tendency is to

only narratives of intrinsic beauty and human value, but they are also historical documentation which the anthropologist, the social historian, and any other specialist may properly scan for evidence about life in Achaean Greece. So, likewise, the nineteenth-century novel can be made to yield an immense mass of evidence about middle-class value systems in Europe and North America without thereby losing its place as the modern equivalent of epic poetry.

make reading and writing more difficult rather than more attractive. Balance rather than bitterness is what is desired. Critics and historians alike are concerned with books or works of art not as they exist materially but as they have meaning, and meaning is forever of two sorts: that which the naïve beholder immediately apprehends, and the richer meaning that can be disengaged from the work only by appropriate aesthetic analysis operating with the aid of relevant historical knowledge. In the words of Erwin Panofsky, from whom the injunction comes: "Archaeological research is blind and empty without aesthetic re-creation, and aesthetic re-creation is irrational and often misguided without archaeological research." [6]

It is, of course, true that the greatest works of art—the Parthenon, Beethoven's final piano sonata, *Hamlet*, "The Burial of Count Orgaz," *The Betrothed* of Manzoni are examples—have an air of escaping from time and occasion and soaring to that abode where the eternal are. It is also true that the naïve reader-spectator-auditor, except in the case of art of such Alexandrian character that unless you belong to the initiated you cannot comprehend it at all, gets a good deal out of works of art without the apparatus of learning. One recalls Dr. Johnson's picture of the boy in the corner reading Shakespeare, stumbling over incomprehensible words, yet fascinated by the tale. It is an attractive, even a romantic, thought to suppose that you can clean the pure, proud face of art of all irrelevancies. But there is no such thing as a pure and absolute present tense. The proposal is fundamentally impossible, and its effect has in the past proved mischievous. Eighteenth-century aesthetic theory, for example, worked out an absolute; one of the results was the ridiculous concept of the barbaric

[6] Erwin Panofsky, *Meaning in the Visual Arts*, Anchor Books, 1955, p. 19. But see the whole first section on the history of art as a humanistic discipline.

Middle Ages. Works of art are made by specific persons laboring in specific times and places to accomplish specific ends, and we cannot know the full import of what they wrought without knowing why and how they set themselves a task and carried it out. "In modern art criticism," wrote Malinowski, "it is customary to regard a work of art as an individual message from the creative artist to his audience, the expression of an emotional or intellectual state translated through the work of art from one man to another. Such a conception is useful only if the whole cultural context and the tradition of art are taken for granted." [7] The comment is that of an anthropologist, but it is verified in the practice of great criticism.

4

There is indeed no more misleading phrase in this context than "the dead hand of the past." Humane learning perpetually points forward. It creates ideas out of dead fact; it vitalizes artifact and document for the use of criticism here and now. It does not reduce art to sociology; rather, it illumines society through art—not the ephemeral society of any given year, but that Great Society central to the philosophic thinking of Josiah Royce. "A drama, a symphony, a painting, a religious ritual, a bank, an army corps," writes Florian Znaniecki, "each has a specific standardized inner order of its own with which all those comply who participate in it directly or vicariously; this order raises it above the arbitrariness and variability of subjective psychological experiences and impulses." [8] It is order of this kind rather than the pure criticism of absolute art that is central both to the practice of art and the character

[7] B. Malinowski, "Culture," *Encyclopaedia of the Social Sciences, sub v.*
[8] *The Social Role of the Man of Knowledge,* Columbia University Press, 1940, p. 192.

of humane learning. But the same writer eloquently puts the matter with even greater force in an earlier page of his book:

The question of the significance of scholarly knowledge for personal intellectual development brings us to what is perhaps the most important historical function of learned schools and scholars. They have initiated and spread in civilized societies the deeply stimulating conviction that man, the individual man, this ephemeral being dependent on his natural milieu for his bodily life and on his social milieu for his spiritual life, can alone and unaided by any divine grace or revelation reach in thought the Absolute, discover the ultimate nature of the world and his own nature. Illusion be it—but a noble illusion! And by no means illusory are its consequences. For if such is the essence of true knowledge, then the possession of true knowledge or even disinterested striving for pure truth gives man a transcendent worth, an inner superiority far above the ignorant and the despiser of knowledge, however powerful and practically influential, however wealthy in worldly goods.[9]

⁹ Znaniecki, *op. cit.*, p. 161. The rest of the passage is also interesting. "No wonder that the genuine scholar is proverbially negligent and forgetful in everyday practical matters, lives in seclusion from political struggles, is satisfied with a very modest economic status. But this does not mean that secular scholarly knowledge makes men unfit for practical life. On the contrary, the man who has successfully striven for pure truth without regard to its practical use and whose knowledge is systematically organized by strictly theoretic standards, if he turns his thought to practical problems, will be better able to solve them than a man who has learned only what he needed for practical purposes." The statement is made in terms of "practicality," which one glosses as business or politics or both. Substitute "art" or "criticism" for "practicality" and, in a general sense, the truth still holds. The discipline of craftsmanship and insight derived from systematic knowledge enhances, it does not kill, creativity in art (pp. 161–162).

NINE

Value Judgments

One of the interesting demands upon the humanities, humane learning, and humanistic scholarship is that they shall teach "value judgments." This phrase is common in educational discussion, especially among academic administrators, who, though they support science and social science, incline to believe these branches of knowledge do not inculcate value judgments, and look to the humanities to redress the imbalance. Laymen also take this point of view. Popular statements run like these: The humanities deal with "worth-while" things, whereas science and social science principally satisfy curiosity and train for jobs. Philosophy shows you what to believe and how to live. Literature is something you ought to study in college because, when you leave, you won't have time to read, reading in this context meaning the analysis of masterpieces under guidance. The study of art and music ("appreciation") is applauded on similar grounds.

Since these flattering statements are echoes of humane opinion, it may at first sight seem surprising that they involve any puzzle. But, to begin with, terms like "value judgments" and "values" are ambiguous. Sometimes they mean nothing more than "worth-while" things. Sometimes they refer, however vaguely, to creating taste and disciplining emotions, "emotional education" being a powerful phrase in pedagogical theory. Sometimes they imply the acquisition of an ethical outlook or of some form of philosophical belief, the assumption being that the study of great books, great art, great religions, and great thinkers can eventuate in nothing less than high moral principles. This nobility of outlook is identified with idealism— hence the wide diffusion of Plato in humanistic teaching— and idealism is conceived to be not only a shield against the materialism of science and the grubbiness of earning a living, but it becomes a treasury upon which to draw in making crucial decisions in after years.

The proud purpose of humane learning is, indeed, the making of a better society composed of nobler men and women, but this task has its perplexities. There is no simple relation between the study of the humanities and the effect of that study. A rich acquaintance with philosophy and the arts has been acquired by various unlovely characters without, apparently, influencing them for the good. Thus the legend concerning Nazi leaders who played the piano exquisitely and simultaneously, as it were, tortured their victims seems to have some foundation in fact. Wide knowledge of thought has led some students into skepticism and others into a general nihilistic outlook. Moreover, important contributions to thought have come from personalities of contradictory qualities. Thus, an important aesthetic theory was produced by Schopenhauer, who was not only a pessimist but something of a misanthrope as well; a powerful thinker like Hume spent his intellectual life undercutting all forms of rationalism; the materialist Lucretius produced a noble poem; a rascal like Villon wrote tender lyrics; and an adventurer like Benvenuto Cellini penned a fascinating autobiography. On the other hand, Machiavelli in private life was prudent and circumspect, yet *The Prince* has created a great deal of mischief in the world. It is of course possible that anomalies cancel out in the general march toward nobility, but these personalities were in their time masters of humanistic learning. In truth, learning can display a disconcerting inconsistency of influence: Porson, Bentley, Aretino, Walter Savage Landor, Nietzsche, Oscar Wilde, and Professor Sir Gilbert Murray all studied Greek, but how various the results!

2

There seem to be four central questions here. 1) What is meant by value judgments? 2) Are administrators and others right in denying "values" or the capacity to inculcate values to science and the social sciences? 3) Are there sources of value judgments the general humanities overlook? 4) How do the humanities induce value judgments, if they do?

What are values? The dictionary definitions do not help us, and we can best understand what is meant if we set up three general statements. 1) Values are expressions of preferences. 2) A value system is a pattern of preferences shared by members of a group. 3) A value judgment is the expression, actual or implied, of a decision to accept (and if necessary act upon) this preference rather than that one. Values cannot exist in a state of anarchy. They are not so many atoms. They have meaning only as an expression of preference. Since I cannot prefer but only accept something that is unique, values, if they exist at all, must exist in clusters. The resulting pattern is defined either by these interrelations or by the relation of the value system to the group that lives in the light of these values, or, more commonly, by both considerations.

The value system latent or expressed in the humanities in American education is inevitably a value system consonant with Western society, a fact that is at once its strength and its weakness. The strength lies in the truth that some possibilities are out of bounds. Thus no amount of exposure to stories and representations of a harem, however seductive, seems likely to persuade Westerners that polygamy is morally preferable to monogamy, though in their sacred book the Old Testament speaks without reproach of polygamy. On the other hand, the persistent concurrence with traditional modes of Western life of the values expressed or latent in "our" humanities is a stumbling block in the way of sympathetically understanding the values of any other sort of society. To transcend the value system of "our" humanities requires a stronger imaginative effort than most Westerners are willing to make.

But we have not yet come to grips with the meaning of values. A value judgment—that is, the announcement, actual or implied, of the decision to accept and, if necessary, act upon a preference—implies a determination to go about validating something, since, in effect, choice is a move toward validation and can be nothing else. I decide to find out the truth about something this way rather than that way, or I decide that such and such an object, piece of music, literary work, or something else yields a higher aesthetic satisfaction than that one, or I decide that this act or course of conduct rather than some other will do me and my group either less harm or more good. My validations—that is, my value judgments—obviously concern 1) knowledge, 2) beauty, and 3) conduct.

3

To deny science and the social sciences the power of acting upon value judgments and of inculcating them is an error that rises from two misconceptions: a misunderstanding of the range and nature of value judgments; and mistaking the part for the whole. The second is obvious: because many technical operations of science and of social science involve impersonality and quantification, it should not be inferred that either science or social science operates without persons and is unable and unwilling to pass from quantitative to qualitative judgments. In social science, indeed, perhaps the leading theoretical question in the field is the question of ameliorative aims versus mere reporting, observation, and mensuration, but even the impersonalists, if one may coin a word, believe they are working for a better science and a better society. What is more important, scientist and scholar alike operate on the assumption that ascertainable truth is better than half-truth, illusion, assertion, or dogma without evidence, perhaps the single most important value judgment that can be made. Each assumes, moreover, that some modes of ascertaining truth are preferable to others. For example, the famous cry of Professor Anton J. Carlson, now part of the folklore of biology, "Vot is de evidence?" implies an important value judgment: it is better to accept an assertion resting upon a substratum of a particular sort of evidence than it is to accept an unsupported assertion, however plausible. Scientist and social scientist, confronted by masses of refractory material and by questions of immense perplexity (the whole composition of the universe is merely one of these), learn in the main a quality of humility of mind that should be widely spread among all intellectual circles. Finally, when a scientist (in contradistinction to certain frightened humanists) talks about the beauty of the universe, that is precisely what he means. He means that its sweep and grandeur, however impersonal, give him a feeling of sublimity like the feeling of sublimity others receive from great music. He may also mean that manifestations of nature revealed by thought, by inspection, or in the laboratory have the precise attractions of art.[1] The doctrine that social science or science is essentially "inhumane" in both senses of that battered word is denied in every tribute to a great scientist or great theorist, tributes as humble and sincere as those paid to great musicians, poets, artists, or philosophers.[2]

One special case of mistaking the part for the whole needs at least passing comment. Conduct *is* three-fourths of life; and moral patterns in conduct are of great professional interest to social scientists, who by and by arrive at the not very novel conclusion that social needs condition morality. In this light, moral systems are by them studied objectively. It is then inferred by careless observers that the social scientists have now reduced morals to relativity —that is, any kind of moral system that works is good, and no kind of moral sanction is valid that does not work. It is next assumed by these same observers that value judgments (in this case, moral ones) are therefore impossible, since morals are always treated objectively. But this is queer argument. In the first place, if there are transcendental sanctions in any moral system, the social scientist simply notes the fact, but he does not deny them. In the second place, the social scientist was not the originator of the theory that value judgments are relative, a doctrine that had its most cutting expositor in Pascal, who observed: Truth on this side the Pyrenees, error on that side. In the third place, in observing that moral systems

[1] See, for example, Paul Weiss, "Beauty and the Beast: Life and the Rule of Order," *Scientific Monthly*, 81(6), 286–299, December, 1955.

[2] Read the sympathetic analysis of Kurt Lewin by Henry S. Kariel, "Democracy Unlimited: Kurt Lewin's Field Theory" in *The American Journal of Sociology*, 62(3), 280–289, November, 1956 or the lengthy, just, and philosophic analysis of Sigmund Freud ("Freud and Psychoanalysis") by David Riesman in *Individualism Reconsidered*, Free Press, 1954, pp. 305–408. But for that matter the whole book is as much a contribution to philosophy as it is to the social sciences.

are relative, the social scientist does not deny that they exist or that they have meaning; in fact, he asserts that so far as he can find out every culture and every society has some sort of morality. Finally, the social scientist does not say either directly or inferentially that either he or anybody else can get along without moral commitment. Doubtless a student of the Kinsey reports will evaluate adultery in a manner shocking to a Scotch Covenanter, but he does not therefore argue that fornication is a matter of entire indifference to everybody. Let his watch be stolen while he is making an opinion survey in the slums, and the social scientist will react with the same emotional violence as anybody else. The capacity to make value judgments is one thing; a belief that unless you assent to a transcendental moral system you have no morality at all is not only quite another thing, but it is a problem in metaphysics and logic, not in social science.

4

Our third question—are there sources of value judgment the general humanities overlook?—leads us at once to religion. In church-controlled schools all value judgments, whether they concern knowledge, beauty, or conduct, can, of course, be referred to acceptable premises in theology. The value system is a closed system, since the answer to even an aesthetic question ("Is this book, picture, or sonata something that will give me the right aesthetic enjoyment?") will in the long run originate in a theological interpretation of beauty and duty. In such a system the obligation of the artist is so to work that both he and his audience will praise God and glorify Him in a manner consonant with the theological system.

Great areas of art and thought in the Western world are intelligible only as we grant, if not a theological, at least a religious context or meaning, assumed, expressed, or inferred. Furthermore, since we in the West live in cultural traditions strongly influenced by Judaeo-Christian values, religious presuppositions govern our tastes even unconsciously and may interfere with a just appreciation of art and thought originating in another culture. For example: a quality of Indic art is multitudinousness, arising presumably from the attempt of the artist, by filling every inch of space with figures, animals, vines, or formal intricacies, to suggest swarming life around him. We in the West, insistent upon individual salvation, whether secular (self-improvement) or theological, are puzzled or repelled by this lack of interest in individuality and must self-consciously adjust ourselves to a novel set of values.[3] Religious influence can be, and is, diffused as a quality in value judgments.

In the beginning, humanism, as we have seen, originated in the impulse to move knowledge out from under theology. In the United States we are dedicated to the separation of church and state. Tax-supported institutions do not teach theology, or, more accurately, do not accept it as dogma, though they may examine theology as a historical phenomenon. Moreover, many church-supported private colleges and universities, even if they maintain a school of theology, require that general instruction go forward on a "liberal" (non-theological) basis. But religion is by no means excluded from values, even if theology be confined. Not only is the Bible taught as "literature," but Christian art and music, though they come under the rubric of art, retain a considerable infusion of religious values even in state-supported institutions.

Americans go even further and expect a general tend-

---

[3] Even so good a critic of art as Bernard Berenson seems unable to make this readjustment, declaring at the close of *Aesthetics and History* that the only true tradition in art originates in the Mediterranean world.

ency of exhortation toward the better things of life from classroom teaching of the humanities in college and, perhaps less frequently, in the universities. This expectation importantly colors value judgments. If every sort of value expressed in the arts were given proportionate weight, it seems at least plausible that Rabelaisianism, paganism, hedonism, cynicism, and selfishness would be as often the result of exposure to the humanities as are altruism, generosity of soul, and social adjustment. In fact, this does not occur. A transfer of something resembling the religious spirit to value systems implicit in the humanities is silently made. The assumption is that the life-enhancing values in Rembrandt, or Shakespeare, or Beethoven are normative and powerful, as against abnormal life-enhancing values in Swinburne, Oscar Wilde, Casanova, or Aretino, the eroticism of *Tristan und Isolde,* the decadence of Strauss' *Salome,* or the allure of lush nudes by Ingres, Titian, Goya, or Manet. Logically, at least, it can be argued that if exposure to the nobility of Milton helps induce nobility in the young, exposure to the Prelude and "Love-Death" of *Tristan und Isolde* will not only fail to inspire nobility but may inspire something else.[4] But this does not commonly occur because humanistic teaching in American schools is still under a moral imperative. Anterior value judgments have been accepted before teaching begins, partly because of the wide acceptance of the view that much reverence is due to youth. On the other hand, the violence and "darkness" of much contemporary fiction from Faulkner to Céline creates awkward problems of value judgments, so that one occasionally wonders whether the critical theory that *Light in August* is, after all, a sort of Christian allegory may not arise from the

[4] Studies like Mario Praz's *The Romantic Agony* and G. Lafourcade's *La Jeunesse de Swinburne* seem to come more easily from European scholars than they do from American ones.

pedagogical desire to avoid saying it is an extremely brutal and even terrifying work of art.

5

It appears then that only a minority of educational institutions systematically refer value judgments to theology, but that a general religious sanction, vague but powerful, operates throughout the area of the humanities wherever problems of value judgments arise. Some may prefer to call this influence ethical, but on the whole its sanctions arise from the Christian ethic, humanists are anxious not to appear to be combating Christianity, and the term "religious" is appropriate and useful. But what of value judgments in the humanities proper? To what are they referred? Here we face one of the queerest paradoxes of academic life. Patently, questions concerning knowledge, beauty, and conduct formally belong to philosophy— knowledge to metaphysics and epistemology, beauty to aesthetics, and conduct to ethical theory. Yet the demand by administrators and others for value judgments is directed to the humanities generally, and not specifically to departments of philosophy, largely because recent and contemporary movements in philosophical departments have called into question the systematic theories that formerly gave rise to value judgments! This curious condition is not caused by any delinquency on the part of philosophers, who are seriously pursuing what seems to them appropriate professional aims. But the present professional aim of many philosophers is not to create systematic thought but to analyze general propositions and modes of communication. Precisely as to be a successful professor of English is one thing and to be a successful novelist is another, so one does not have to be a philosopher to secure a Ph.D. in philosophy, if by "philosopher" one has in view what Wordsworth meant when he wrote of the years that bring the philosophic mind. Departments of philosophy are commonly less concerned with wisdom than they are with refining and sharpening communication among branches of knowledge. This is a highly necessary task, but it has meant that the tradition of wisdom has been referred to the totality of humane learning rather than to departments of philosophy. This does not mean that the country lacks philosophers of sagacity and judgment; it does mean that until the tide turns (there are signs of its turning), philosophical experts are more likely to argue that "This is red" really means "This appears to me as red" and then proceed to analysis of the second statement (Why "appears"? What or who is meant by "me"? What does anybody mean by "red"?) than they are to build up notions of the true, the beautiful, and the good. "The uneasy state of contemporary philosophy," writes Kathleen Nott, "comes from its attempt to identify philosophy with logic, and logic with deductive or purely analytical logic . . . this is perhaps the consequence of a failure to recognize that language is primarily a means of communication rather than of description." [5] This echoes Professor William K. Frankena's earlier observation that philosophers have talked of ethical theory "as if the focus were ethical words and sentences and as if the object were to know what these semantically mean. This has perhaps made for a certain sterility." [6]

Although great teachers continue to discourse sagely and sympathetically about masters of thought from Plato to Dewey, presenting whatever elements in their views still retain significance for thoughtful men, it is nevertheless true of philosophy as of religion that its influence has been

[5] "The Study of Man: A British Critic Views the Scene," *Commentary*, 24:454–460, November, 1957.

[6] "Moral Philosophy at Mid-Century," *The Philosophical Review*, 60:44–45, January, 1951.

diffused over the whole area of the humanities. This diffusion has come about from a variety of causes other than an alleged sterility in philosophy proper. When historians gave up the theory that history is only past politics, they came to the notion of cultural history. But cultural history requires that students interest themselves in the climates of opinion of particular times and places, and this in turn requires them to discuss philosophy. The growth of the concept of intellectual history (history of ideas) is another mode of this deepening. In the teaching of literature few scholars today are satisfied with knowing only the external facts of a work—its author, its date, its sources, its occasion, its bibliographical fortunes—they dwell on the ideational contents and the moral and aesthetic qualities of book, play, and poem. If the same emphasis is not immediately evident in the graphic arts and in music, it is only because sight and sound have here to be translated into words, whereas in literature words are both the substance of art and the means of explicating it.

Conceivably present trends in philosophical thinking may even not be so remote from the problem of value judgments as unkind critics imply. Few mature expounders of any humanistic discipline try to impose a general value system on their students; they seek, rather, to make clear why some set of value preferences, however inconsistent or even unconscious in part the system may be, is requisite for maturing mind and the emotions. A poem is not beautiful in proportion as it is Catholic or Protestant, a painting is not "true to life" because it is realistic or ideal, a sonata does not acquire permanent worth merely because it is Russian or American. Works of art and systems of thought speak to men and women as human beings, not to New Critics, Seventh-day Adventists, economic royalists or dwellers in skid row. The first step in making value judgments in the humanities is to learn to estimate beauty (or knowledge or conduct) by standards arising from and applicable to beauty (or knowledge or conduct), not by standards imposed on beauty (or knowledge or conduct) from extraneous forces. We recognize this truth whenever we turn up our democratic noses at official art in, say, Russia, but we forget all about it whenever local prejudice insists upon destroying the new mural in the post office because it is "un-American," or whenever sentimental defenders of minority groups denounce *The Merchant of Venice, Huckleberry Finn,* or *Uncle Tom's Cabin* as bad art because these books are unkind to Jews, Negroes, or Southerners. Understanding the concept that art has its special values is the beginning of wisdom in value judgments.[7]

6

A second element in nourishing capacity for value judgments in the humanities is the realization that a masterpiece has been there for a long, long time. This does not mean it will forever be classed as masterly, nor does it mean that everybody has to like every masterpiece. But odds are on the side of the masterpiece, not on the side of the private disliker. When, after thoughtful consideration of the masterpiece—its time, its organization, its substance, its style, its purpose—the student still finds that this particular masterpiece says nothing to him, he may properly ticket it for a time as "Unacceptable," but he must learn not to ticket it as "Incompetent," "Counterfeit," "Stupid," or "Not Up-to-date," any more than he may ticket Kant a sham, *Die Meistersinger* a failure, or Richardson a Sunday-school novelist because Kant, Wagner, and Richardson do not on a particular date in a particular set of circumstances speak directly to the interest of the student. One ought

[7] This is not the same thing as the art-for-art's-sake theory.

always to keep in mind the wild and wonderful image in Emerson's prose of the universe looking quietly down and asking: "Why so hot, little man?" In condemning whole systems of thought and schools of art one is more likely to reveal one's own lack of civilization than one is to reveal the lack of modern civilization in masterpieces.

7

A third important component in the problem is to realize what blood, sweat, and tears it requires of artist and thinker and scholar to create the masterpieces that seem smoothly to emerge from nowhere. American educational critics sometimes speak and write as if the only task requiring infinite care is technical invention. A Gregor Mendel patiently crossing sweet peas in a monastery garden has drawn, it is true, some respectful references, but a Gibbon toiling almost thirty years to put together *The Decline and Fall of the Roman Empire,* a Marx sitting day after day in the British Museum and taking notes, and more notes, and still more notes, a Rodin designing and redesigning his great, unfinished work "The Portals of Hell," a Beethoven continually rethinking musical themes until they soar out of the commonplace into the empyrean, and all this amid growing deafness, a Darwin opening his first notebook in 1837 and laboring until 1859 to publish a classic of literature and of science, *The Origin of Species* —these instances suggest that reverence may be due to others than golf champions, TV comedians, night-club singers, and those who, though they may toil, leave little behind them. There is no virtue in toil as such. But Verdi, producing at eighty the vivacious music of *Falstaff,* is not only as professionally skilled as any tennis coach, he creates lasting pleasure for all mankind. If these examples seem a little elementary, they are directed against the common fallacy that art is play ("worthy leisure-time activities"), scholarship the work of men who "never met a payroll," and thought something you can get out of a digital computer, a staff conference, or a sales analysis.

The artist knows better. After a good many years as a child prodigy, Yehudi Menuhin decided that he ought to understand the music he had been playing. He said:

In making this decision to realign my musical values . . . my mind had to measure and reinforce the promptings of my heart, leading me in my late adolescence to seek a reason for the values I had sensed in Beethoven, Bach and other great musicians. . . . The most significant result was to me the acquisition of the *knowledge* of something which I had previously *felt,* namely, that all great musical works have a unity, structural and expressive, an organic relationship of parts toward each other and toward the whole. This unity found its consummation in Bach, and most revealing to me, in his six *Sonatas and Partitas for the Violin Alone.* In them, as in a conception of Leonardo da Vinci, science, mysticism and art are blended in a Holy Trinity. The harmony and unity of those Bach works are such that each sequence is akin to a sculpture fitted into a niche which, in turn, forms part of the nave of a cathedral, the cathedral itself planned as an integral part of a square in the heart of a city which blends with the surrounding countryside.

The profundity of a mind may be measured by the extent to which it sees universal phenomena as part of a vast whole, and not merely as the indulgence of a benign deity or the work of an evil genius bent on pranks. The more completely one sees a process or an event in its inevitability, the more fully one has comprehended it, and the more truthfully and inspiringly one is able to recreate it in a work of art. Only a great mind, such as Da Vinci's or Albert Einstein's, would conceive and execute the unity and harmony that had gone into the creation of Bach's *Sonatas and Partitas for the Violin Alone.*[8]

One may know nothing about the six sonatas and be unable to comprehend what Menuhin says, but one of the value judgments to be found in the humanities is respect for the human mind.

8

These are casual examples of phases of the value problem. Because value judgments run from the infinite variety of thought and art to the infinite variety of men and women, and not from approved art and official thought to patriotic, right-thinking admirers of Big Brother, it is impossible to lay down rules. All kinds of principles from philosophy, psychology, pedagogy, good citizenship, and ethics can rise portentously at this point and frighten off the timid. It is, moreover, difficult to distinguish between making value judgments about the humanities and making value judgments within the humanities. Perhaps it is unnecessary to do so, since the mere existence of the humanities is a value judgment in itself. It is not quite true to say that in the humanities one man's meat is another man's poison, but it is probably true that, within limits, there is no disputing about tastes. If it be true that everyone is born either a Platonist or an Aristotelian, it sometimes seems true that everyone comes to the humanities already a romantic, a realist, an existentialist, a pragmatist, a mystic, a hedonist, or a Hegelian. But none of this can be construed to mean that bad taste does not differ from good taste, dubious conduct is on the same plane as honorable

[8] Robert Magidoff, *Yehudi Menuhin*, Doubleday, 1955, pp. 200–201. Musicians will be interested in the analysis of key relations among the six sonatas which follows. In this connection the phonograph record made on the conductor's eightieth birthday, "Bruno Walter in Conversation with Arnold Michaelis," Columbia Masterworks, is important.

conduct, and logical fallacies are indifferent to the believer in truth and virtue. The moderns admire a Hemingway with his private code of honor. Perhaps the best thing that can be said of the humanities is that, properly understood and taught, they permit civilized man to form his private code of honor.

Where man is not, said William Blake, nature is barren. Men are not helped in daily living if they concentrate their gaze upon what some of the moderns are pleased to think of as an inhuman universe. Conduct *is* three-fourths of life, and conduct is, but in no didactic sense, the theme of humane learning. The humanities concern life itself in all its variety, or, more accurately, how life has been lived on this planet, and how it could be lived. The report is given by some of the best and happiest minds mankind has ever known. Its themes are the search for happiness, the contemplation of death, the search for truth, the meaning of beauty. The works of art and thought that make up the substance of humane learning have to do with love, the nature of loyalty, cowardice, heroism, treason, remorse, gladness, the effects of faith and of the loss of faith, the meaning of domestic life, the drive of passions, the significance of nature and of the sound of music, and the relation of time to eternity. Conduct is seldom influenced by rule, but by experience and example. Example and vicarious experience are possible in and through humane learning, and so it is that a private code of honor can be hammered out. Philosophy and ethics interpret experience, art presents it. Both are in the domain of the humanities.

Present fashions in criticism and philosophy celebrate frustration and disaster. But these, if life survives, will, like other fashions of the world, pass by, leaving the drama of heroism and compassion once more unobscured. The virtue of the present age, though we are loathe to admit it, is compassion, but the meaning of charity, that greatest of the trinity in Paul's epistle, it is the intention of humane studies to enrich. The weakness of the present hour is its failure to sound the heroic note, but heroism is pictured in the humanities, heroism is infectious, and heroism needs to be rediscovered, whether it be found in the mystical death of an Oedipus at Colonnos or in the brassier but still inspiriting concept of Macaulay:

> And how can men die better
> Than facing fearful odds
> For the ashes of their fathers
> And the altars of their gods.

No amount of statistical analysis will re-enforce love of country, no amount of psychiatric lore alter the truth of Juliet's love for young Romeo. Men are not moved by digital calculators, but by color and example. Moreover, if we are to retain civilization, we must lay hold upon those who have been civilized; and those who have been civilized are those who have created the humanities. In encouraging right value judgments, humanism, without prejudice to the churches, still makes a central value judgment for all mankind, best phrased by William Blake when he wrote: "The worship of God is: Honouring his gifts in other men, each according to his genius, and loving the greatest men best."

3. Some Practical Issues

TEN

What to Expect
from the Humanities

We have wandered from the questions with which this book began, but the discussion has brought some light to bear on at least some of them, such as: "Why is it that you think the humanities are so important? Do the humanities make people better? Do they make people happier? Do they make people more capable? How do you know?" Perhaps nobody knows how to make any human being better, happier, or more capable, but at the very least the humanities, humane learning, and humanistic scholarship help to sustain a universe of thought in which these questions have meaning and in which adult minds may have opportunity to work out such problems for themselves.

Our businessman asked: "What can the humanities do for me, for my family, for my business, for my community?" This question, too, has been partially answered. But let us take another look at these, and related, inquiries and their implications. Perhaps one of the causes for the misunderstanding of the humanities, humane learning, and humanistic scholarship is that these questions, honest though they are, may be misleading, or at least lead to expectations that are misleading, so that the true nature and function of the humanities are not clearly grasped.

Let us go back to the original set of inquiries and substitute "science" for the humanities and see what happens.

The questions "What is science? Why do you think it important? What can science do for me, for my family, for my business, for my community? Does science make people better, happier, more capable? What is the best way for the business world to help science? Can science be applied to business?" become rhetorical only. The concept of science and the scientist offers no problem to most Americans. A scientist is a man engaged either in scientific investigations or in working at the application of scientific discoveries to industry, the art of war, improvements in medicine, and so on. Even if the questioner could not define science to the satisfaction of philosophers, he can define it well enough for the business community. Science is a way of understanding the world and a way of operating on the nature of things so that, by controlling or inducing change,[1] you help mankind. Of course science benefits business and the community, the family and the individual, and of course the community and business should support science, which they do.

To substitute social science for science in these same questions produces somewhat more mixed results, but on the whole the response is like that aroused by science. Uncertainty, where it appears, seems to rise from two sources: American opinion of the social sciences is not quite so affirmative as is American opinion of science; and the term itself is less definite in the public mind. On an elementary level social science may even be identified with socialism and repudiated, and on a more advanced plane there lingers some confusion between sociology and the social

[1] Consider this characteristic pronouncement by Charles F. Kettering of General Motors: "There are no places where anyone can sit down and rest in an industrial situation. It is a question of change, change, change, all the time—and it is always going to be that way. It must always be that way for the world only goes along one road, the road to progress." Quoted in James W. Prothro, *The Dollar Decade,* Louisiana State University Press, 1954, p. 86.

worker. As, however, it is commonly agreed that social work is a good thing, no harm is done to the social sciences. If one substitutes for the generic "social scientist," more specific terms like economist, political scientist, social anthropologist, and so on, these experts seem to share the general American approval of *expertise* and may on occasion receive the accolade of contributing to prosperity.

Approval of science and in lesser degree of social science permits the experts to be unintelligible to the layman. The American does not expect to understand the exact nature of scientific research so long as he feels the results are going to be beneficial; and, this being true, he is quite willing that the language in which results are published shall be unintelligible—the privilege of *expertise*. Complaint is sometimes made about the jargon of social science, but on the whole the social scientist is also allowed to speak and write like an expert. The vocabulary of business administration is in part identical with the language of economics; and, moreover, the Americans, impressed by the dark vocabulary of psychology, are willing to assume that social psychologists, sociologists, and others like them know what they are talking about. Their approval rests upon the assumption that science and, in lesser degree, the social sciences induce change, change is progress, and progress is a law of life. If change is not induced, change can at least be beneficially measured, as in the statement: "While in 1820 we were obliged to keep 71.8 per cent of our working population engaged in agriculture to feed the rest, today (in 1950) 11.6 per cent of our working population engaged in agriculture can feed themselves and the remaining 88.4 per cent as well." [2] Behind statistical analysis, of which this sentence is a simple instance, there lies a technical vocabulary of words like mean, median, and

[2] David M. Potter, *People of Plenty*, University of Chicago Press, 1954, p. 89.

skew curve, which do not, apparently, trouble the layman. He expects or tolerates this professional speech because these experts "get results." They "do something" for himself, his business, his family, and his community.

2

In the area of the humanities things queerly alter. In the first place, the humanities profess to deal directly with human nature, not as the psychologist or the physiologist or the sociologist does, but plainly, and generally. Their basic assumption is that across the ages and in all lands there appears the common denominator, Man. Their proponents talk about the universality of literature and the other arts, they proclaim that the pursuit of philosophy is part of wisdom, and they declare that language is one of man's proudest inventions and that every educated person should write and talk simply, elegantly, and well. Surely, then, that which is general should be so expressed that it can be generally understood—how else shall we arrive at universal teaching? Yet humanistic scholarship seems to deny its very premise. Discussing the language of poetry, it can produce sentences like this:

If we look back at the prosodic devices found in the poetic texts discussed in this chapter (word parallelism, onomato-poeization, rhyme, anaphora, etc.), we are struck by the variety of phenomena which can however be reduced to one basic phenomenon: symbolic *repetition of sound elements,* connotative of identities or homologies in outward reality, which is already given in language as such but is expanded in poetry.[3]

What in the world is the man talking about? Why doesn't he tell us what he means? The gulf between language of this sort and the language of "favorite poems," such as

[3] Leo Spitzer, "Language of Poetry," in *Language: An Enquiry into Its Meaning and Function,* Harper, 1957, p. 229.

> Take up our quarrel with the foe:
> To you from failing hands we throw
>   The torch; be yours to hold it high.
>   If ye break faith with us who die
> We shall not sleep, though poppies grow
>   In Flanders fields

is immense. And though the difference is, in fact, no greater than that between the language of the common man and that in which scientific discussion is carried on,[4] the technical vocabulary of humanistic scholarship, of literary criticism, of metaphysics, and of other great areas of humane learning is labeled pedantic. Humanistic scholarship is not only denied the right granted scientists and social scientists to be unintelligible to laymen, but it is also expected to be immediately understood by the common reader.

Doubtless scholarly prose could be improved, and so doubtless could the prose of science and of social science, but that is another problem. The fundamental difficulty is that the privilege of *expertise* in the case of humanistic scholarship has been silently altered or denied. All specialization, however, requires a special vocabulary and cannot go forward without one. This does not mean that everybody concerned with the humanities must perforce be a specialist speaking to specialists only. It does mean that, just as one distinguishes between the desirability of clear, simple, and persuasive teaching in elementary science courses and courses in social sciences, and the need of experts in these fields to pursue special work and express their findings in technical terms, untrammeled by demands for popularization, so one must also distinguish

---

[4] Consider, as an example, this relatively simple statement by Niels Bohr: "The attempt at developing a consistent account of electromagnetic and optical phenomena revealed, however, that observers moving relative to each other with great velocities will coordinate events differently." (*The Unity of Knowledge*, ed. by Lewis Leary, Doubleday, 1955, p. 49.)

between the desirability of simple and persuasive teaching (or of popularization) in the humanities and the need of the humanist to follow his research wherever it goes and to present his results in the language of his specialty. The two functions of humane learning must not be confused.

The point is so important that, even at the risk of repetition, it is worth elaborating. Granted that the humanistic scholar is entitled to a professional vocabulary when he is writing for an audience of his kind, what have we a right to expect when he is addressing the general public? He must write and speak like a cultivated man of learning. His prose should not, in the supposed interests of "teaching" and "appreciation," approach a babyish simplicity that glides over the real difficulty of the subject, but he must avoid the jargon of his trade, he must pitch his exposition at the level of cultivated readers and hearers, not the level of newspaper skimming and idle reading in the "mass magazines." We shall come to the problem of style in another connection; suffice it here to say that so characteristic a product of humane learning as Erich Auerbach's *Mimesis* offers no difficulties to any educated reader. The man of learning has, moreover, one advantage commonly denied the scientist in that he may legitimately suffuse what he writes with his own personality, whereas reports on scientific research are supposed to be as impersonal as possible. The common reader has legitimate complaint if the humanist writes with the deadpan impersonality of a medical journal, just as he has legitimate complaint if the net result of humane learning is to make reading more difficult in cultivated circles rather than more attractive. The guiding principle is, or should be: Does humane learning in this instance make art (or philosophy) more challenging, more interesting, more significant to me as an educated person?

3

A second misconception may arise from the temporal relations, so to speak, among the three great categories of knowledge. Science, in the common meaning of the term, is primarily concerned with present event. The history of science is of small concern to the laboratory technician, who either turns it over to the historian or the philosopher as part of the humanities, or views it as a series of excellent tries at truth, each of which exists principally to be surpassed by later and better equipped technicians. Likewise, the concern of a large portion of the social sciences is with the patterns of living societies.[5]

The substance of the humanities, however, is mostly composed of great masterpieces of thought and art that came into being in past time and cannot be fully understood except in their historical context. These, to be sure, it is the delight of the humanist to interpret to the present student, but because a masterpiece is seldom recognizable at the instant of creation and is, rather, something that has to take on the patina of age, the humanist tends to view current art and thought with a certain reserve. His official abode is, moreover, the museum or the university library, commonly thought of as mausoleums for the mighty dead, whereas the physicist in the radiation laboratory or the economist in the government bureau trying to predict or forestall a business recession is in the very whirl of current problems. Meanwhile, the living artist, thirsty for official recognition, finds, or thinks he finds, the interest of a supposedly powerful professional class eternally directed

[5] See in this connection Howard Mumford Jones, "A Humanist Looks at Science," in *Daedalus: Journal of the American Academy of Arts and Sciences,* Winter, 1958, pp. 102–110.

toward the achievements of the past; and the common reader, concerned with the current book, the present issue, the new creation, is puzzled by the apparent indifference of humanistic experts to living art and thought. Mistrust and misunderstanding inevitably arise. They commonly take shape in an architectural metaphor: the humanistic scholar is implored to get out of his ivory tower, whereas the chemist is paid to stay in his laboratory. It is, of course, not true that scholarship has no interest in current thought or current creativity, but it is certainly true that this interest must perforce be limited. If the scholars were to devote themselves to current thought or current creativity only, who would interpret the masterpieces? Who would bring us the delight, the wonder, the wisdom of the past?

The present does not lack its proponents among us. In the arts, of course, the problem is paradoxical: musical programs are more heavily fraught with past masterpieces than they are with the compositions of living men, and museums more often buy the productions of the past than they do the productions of the present. In the world of literature, or at least of books, the situation is more or less reversed, and the latest novelty gets more acclaim and reading by the general public than do the literary classics. Since there is nobody else to do the work of the scholar, it seems on the whole fair to insist that he do his own job well. On the other hand, antiquarianism among the humanities has long since diminished, the interest of museums in living art is evident, and the playing of contemporary music by established orchestras has been an American practice since the days of Theodore Thomas. Scholar-critics and scholar-teachers by no means lack interest in living poets, novelists, dramatists, and critics, as any search of scholarly periodicals will quickly reveal. Undoubtedly there is considerable confusion now (as always) between "good books" and "literature," between "pictures" and "art," and between tuneful compositions and the more demanding works of living musicians of first rank. The issue is, in sum, slightly factitious; and there is no period in the history of American learning when the interest of humanistic scholarship and humane learning in contemporary art has been livelier than it is at the present time. One can only repeat the caution: If scholarship abandons the explication of the past, who will take it up?

4

A third misconception, particularly evident in higher education, may be called the operational misunderstanding. True it is that the formal purpose of education in science, the social sciences, and the humanities is the philosophical one of understanding man and the universe, or, more accurately perhaps, man in the universe. If this admirable ideal could be fully carried out, we should indeed be a nation of philosophers, but practical considerations intervene. In the spring of any year any university campus is flooded with representatives of business, industry, and, more rarely, government seeking to hire young chemists, young psychologists, young engineers, young technicians of every sort; and though it is universally recognized that a liberal education is theoretically, and even practically, a good thing, the emphasis in job interviews is not on philosophy. The senior knows that he (or she) will shortly have to earn a living in a competitive society—if not in business, then in teaching, or in television, or in social work, or as a newspaper reporter, or a receptionist. Training counts. No amount of excellent admonition alters the brute fact that most undergraduate education is conditioned by vocational desires. Phrases like "the training of engineers," "prelegal training," "teacher training," "the training of junior executives" and so on importantly color the Platonic concept of education.

The interest of business, industry, and government in education cannot be dismissed as merely selfish, inasmuch as business, industry, and government annually pay out millions to support education almost as an act of faith, but it is nevertheless true that business, industry, and government look on academic institutions as sources for the trained personnel they need for an increasing number of specialized and technical jobs. We have as a nation passed beyond the stage when George Horace Lorimer's *Letters of a Self-Made Merchant to His Son* could make endless fun of the dreamy world of the college, but this is in part because the George Horace Lorimer of today has discovered a high degree of practicality in college training. The cynic might say it costs him less; the optimist can declare it is better training than business itself can offer.

What is the role of the humanities, viewed from this angle of vision? Let us stick to a representative case. Of all the branches of humane learning, it is probable that the study of English is the most widely known and the most misunderstood. This misunderstanding illustrates the operational misconception. What good is "English" as a component of these patterns of training? Again and again, after canonical tributes to the honorific but vague notion of "broadening" the student, business leaders, sincerely desirous to do their bit for the humanities, announce in conferences between executives and educational leaders that the "English" written by young businessmen is bad, that it is the duty of teachers of English to see that they write better, that to this end grammar, punctuation, and spelling are essential, and that, insofar as they fail to equip the future businessman with these desirable tools, English departments fail.

Here is a half-truth. That grammar (though not in the business sense of the word), punctuation, and spelling have to be learned and therefore taught by somebody is certain. This would seem to be partly the responsibility of parents, partly the responsibility of the grade school, and partly the function of secondary education, including such vocational institutions as the business college and the secretarial school. But that the primary function of the humanist in college or university is with the simplicities of writing, punctuating, and spelling is simply not true. These matters do not belong in higher education. Yet courses of elementary instruction in the rudiments of composition are a commonplace on the American campus, and the business executive may be pardoned if he assumes they are properly there as training courses.

Two notions of "writing" are here confused. The rudiments of the language, like elementary arithmetic, rudimentary geography, or the elements of history, should have been mastered long before college. Being mastered, they can, of course, flower into something better than conventional correctness, provided the will exists in the student so to develop, and provided the cultural setting of his single-minded enterprise is of the right sort. It is, however, commonplace to observe that the whole man writes. Writing is not a "skill" like skating or running a typewriter; it is a totality of expression involving not only the speech habits of the individual who writes but also the existence of a verbal environment less bare than the language of television shows, the conversation in comic strips, and the colloquial street-corner speech of urban youth. To suppose that a single course in composition during the initial college year, meeting 150 or 200 minutes a week for, say, thirty-six weeks can, in the case of an average American freshman, reverse the slovenly linguistic habits of the past sixteen, seventeen, or eighteen years is to expect the impossible. One does not, one cannot, learn to "write" by taking a single course in English composition; only long exposure to the humanities, only the private discovery that mastering the art of communication is in the long run half the battle even in the social sciences, only the translation of a demand for exactitude in scientific work into the discovery that some degree of a different sort of exactitude is also possible in "writing"—only thus can maturity of style through constant practice be obtained.[6] The totality of impression made by the humanities upon the student is in truth a basic condition for progress toward style; but to suppose that a single course can perform this miracle is to fall into the operational fallacy.

The humanities, rightly understood, are philosophical discourse, not "training." They furnish a point of view; they do not give out "tools" and "skills" like premiums. They cannot weave the silk purse of linguistic elegance from the sow's ear of verbal slovenliness. If the implied indictment seems harsh, let the doubter listen with a critical ear to the American radio, read with a critical eye the magazines on American newsstands, examine with a critical mind the attitude of his contemporaries toward reading, and ponder the truth that Americans read fewer books per capita in proportion to their population than do the citizens of any other great country in the Western world.

5

It would be tedious to analyze other examples of the operational fallacy in the popular concept of the humanities. Logic will not make you "smarter," a course in philosophy will not turn you immediately into a profound thinker, exposure to American history cannot of itself

[6] As Alfred North Whitehead somewhere says: "Style, in its finest sense, is the last acquirement of the educated mind. . . . It pervades the whole being." It takes but a moment to see that "better English" in the world of business is as much a problem of style in this total sense as is the writing of *Paradise Lost*.

guarantee a purer patriotism, nor will enrollment in music appreciation necessarily improve your capacity to carry a tune. Let us turn, therefore, to a somewhat subtler misconception about the humanities—what may be called the misconception of immediate measurement. In one way this is an extension of the operational fallacy; in another sense we confront a genuine difficulty in the claim of humanistic research for support.

All research is theoretically undertaken to satisfy intellectual curiosity and may legitimately claim to be "useless"; *i.e.*, to have no immediate practical application. Inquiries in symbolic logic, the creation of new mathematical puzzles, speculation on the origin of the galaxies, questions about the meaning of right-handedness and left-handedness, or an inquiry into court costumes of the Hittite Empire are examples of "useless" research. It is true that a line of development has led from certain abstruse mathematical statements to the disturbing fact that the Russians explode atomic bombs, just as it is true that the publication in a learned journal of the notebooks of Samuel Taylor Coleridge led eventually to John Livingston Lowe's book *The Road to Xanadu,* a publication that throws more light on literary imagination than does any other scholarly work of the century. But the mathematicians did not invent their formulas to alter international diplomacy, and the scholar who reproduced with painstaking accuracy the cryptic entries in Coleridge's journal could not foresee Professor Lowe's interpretation of the document. Hence research work is commonly justified on the ground that you never can tell what is going to turn up, and therefore you had better let the experts alone. Of course, what the expert does must have some rational relation to knowledge in the field in which he works.[7]

[7] The line between legitimate curiosity and obvious futility is not easy to draw. No one is nowadays much exercised over a problem that gravely

To the common man, however, research commonly implies scientific research. It calls up an image of a laboratory and its physical paraphernalia. Research in the social sciences, he understands, involves a good deal of work with tabulating machines, questionnaires, graphs, curves, and statistics. It is something like a bank. That the humanities may also depend upon research he is willing to grant formally, but he is more than vague, he is really blank, about this mysterious enterprise. Professor So-and-So, specialist in Latin literature of the lower empire, is, he is told, a profoundly learned individual, but how the professor got that way the common man does not know except that he did something mysterious with books, journals, and manuscripts. How can one measure Professor So-and-So's accomplishment? Newspapers and magazines print feature articles about launching an artificial satellite, they record grants of millions of dollars to the Atomic Energy Commission, they carry articles and advertisements by large corporations telling why they subsidize research laboratories for the benefit of business, industry, and mankind. Here is a kind of practical endorsement, a form of measurement, so to say, of the value of research; and this endorsement, this measurement seem to apply particularly to the exact sciences and the social sciences, but not to the humanities. Museums are also built and libraries dedicated, and these events are made public events, but museums and libraries seem, as it were, static affairs compared with the excitement of computing machines and cyclotrons. The completion of a great work of scholarship like H. C. Lancaster's *History of French Dramatic Literature*

concerned the schoolmen and some of their successors: Did Adam have a navel? Since he was not born of woman, he didn't need one; but since he is a "type of Christ" and physically perfect, how could he avoid having one? On the other hand, investigation of the history of this, to us, silly controversy sheds light on an important number of pictures and engravings of Adam and Eve before and after the fall.

in the Seventeenth Century therefore goes unnoticed in the press, whereas newspapers assign specially trained reporters to the annual meetings of the American Association for the Advancement of Science, the publication of a volume of dry statistical analysis like Kinsey's *Sexual Behavior of the Human Male* sets off a vast controversy, and the economic theories of John Maynard Keynes are still keenly debated.

It will be said at once that the Kinsey book affects morals and opinion and Keynesian theory determines policy, and this is true. Each measures or proposes social change. Each also comes to a sort of term, or conclusion. So, likewise, in scientific research it is usually possible to measure distance and result: a Paul Ehrlich tries 605 times to discover a cure for syphilis, and on the six hundred and sixth try he comes up with salvarsan. After enough trials we shall, the theory runs, control cancer as we now control smallpox, or get to the moon as we now traverse the air. The necessary research will at length terminate, the change desired can be effectuated,[8] and we can turn to other problems. But philosophers never reach a conclusion, artists are never satisfied, scholars continue to grumble, folklorists never cease collecting, the interpreters of Shakespeare in one generation tear up the work of their predecessors. Research in the humanities goes round and round; research in science and in the social sciences is much more likely to come to conclusions.

The business corporation is therefore ready to subsidize research in chemistry or economics or the behavioral sciences not merely for the vulgar purpose of avoiding taxes or for the selfish purpose of acquiring new gadgets,

[8] An interesting example of research directed toward change I owe to Dr. Ralph Tyler, who points out that formerly cattle were bred so that cows would produce milk with a high butterfat content. Now that oleomargarine is supplanting butter, cows are being bred to produce milk having a low butterfat content and a high protein value.

but also for the reason that the aim of research in these areas is understandable, its products are both measurable and terminable and can be put into such specific form as this statement: The Palomar telescope collects light originating 350 million light-years away from us, farther than any other telescope ever plunged into space. But the business corporation does not commonly subsidize an international congress of numismatists, an institute for the study of Byzantine culture, or the Modern Language Association of America. And this is largely because, in contrast with the drama of science and the alluring possibilities of social prediction and control, humanistic scholarship makes no showing. Even if it is not wholly occupied with the past, it seems mainly occupied with the past; and, though you may alter the interpretation of the past, history remains a one-way process. You cannot induce change in past events in the sense that science and social science directly or indirectly induce change in conduct or policy in present society. The same measurements cannot apply. When there is no measurement, there can be no estimate of cost, of value, of result. Consequently a kind of puzzled indifference comes over even highly intelligent laymen when the problem of support for humanistic research comes up. What problems are these fellows trying to solve? What policy do they wish to affect? If you give them money, all that happens is that they ask for more money.

Comment on the "misconception of immediate measurement" will here take two forms. In the first place, the American measurement of practicality, finality, applicability, or terminability—whatever term one prefers—is, so to speak, a novelty in intellectual history, and though it is conceivable that all preceding ages have been mistaken, it is also conceivable that the doctrine of immediate measurement may be shallow. The great educational foundations of past centuries have been almost without limit of expectation. Rulers from Augustus and Charlemagne to George II, who chartered the University of Göttingen in 1736, and Friedrich Wilhelm of Prussia, who chartered the University of Berlin in 1809, have been more concerned to create centers of continuing intellectual activity than to require scholars and scientists to stand and deliver. Wealthy benefactors of learning and science, from William of Wykeham to John D. Rockefeller, have on the whole refused to hamper inquiry. The statement attributed to Ezra Cornell, that in founding a university he wanted to create a place where anybody could find instruction in any subject, is truer in essence to the spirit of inquiry in the Western tradition than is the doctrine of the measurable result. Perhaps a famous paragraph by the philosopher Charles Sanders Peirce is here relevant:

In all its progress science vaguely feels that it is only learning a lesson. The value of *Facts* to *it*, lies only in this, that they belong to Nature; and Nature is something great, and beautiful, and sacred, and eternal, and real—the object of its worship and its aspiration. It herein takes an entirely different attitude towards facts from that which Practice takes. For Practice, facts are arbitrary forces with which it has to reckon and to wrestle. Science, when it comes to understand itself, regards facts as merely the vehicles of eternal truth, while for Practice they remain the obstacles which it has to turn, the enemy of which it is determined to get the better. Science, feeling that there is an arbitrary element in its theories, still continues its studies, confident that so it will gradually become more and more purified from the dross of subjectivity; but practice requires something to go upon, and it will be no consolation to it to know that it is on the path to objective truth—the actual truth it must have, or when it cannot attain certainty, must at least have high probability, that is, must know that, though a few of its ventures may fail, the bulk of them will succeed.[9]

[9] From *The Collected Papers of Charles Sanders Peirce*, V:589; quoted in W. B. Gallie, *Peirce and Pragmatism*, Penguin Books, 1952, p. 88.

It may, of course, be objected that Peirce is talking about nature, science, and "facts" from the pragmatic point of view, but the objection is essentially beside the point. Whether this passage means by "science" any and all forms of organized knowledge or "science" in the sense of the physical and natural sciences, the important thing is that even the founder of pragmatism, usually thought to be the American philosophy par excellence, insists that the value of inquiry is not measured by immediately measurable results.[10]

In the second place, and from a quite different point of view, humane learning, far from being static, vague, and ineffective, has been throughout the history of the West one of the principal agents of change, so that, in an odd way, if change is a measure of success in research activity, humanists have overpowering claim to support! Consider what the history of the world would have been if there had been no Greeks, or if we in the United States had never heard of them, or if the humanists of the Renaissance had turned their backs upon Hellas and their faces toward the literature of Germany and Scandinavia. The rediscovery and reinterpretation of the ancient world by Mediterranean scholars in the fifteenth century inaugurated a profound alteration in culture. Research into modes of establishing correct texts in Greek, Latin, and Hebrew altered men's attitudes toward the Bible and was one of the principal causes of the Protestant Reformation. The French philosopher Descartes, meditating upon human reason and the classical geometry of Euclid, began a new phase in thought and helped shape both modern inquiry and the modern world, including the stream of ideas out of which the American constitution was born. When

---

[10] In the same way the distinction between the "pragmatism" of James and the "pragmaticism" of Peirce, fundamental for an understanding of their differences, is irrelevant in this context.

eighteenth-century humanists like the poet Thomas Gray began to find special charm in Scandinavian legend, and nineteenth-century philologists like Franz Bopp and Jacob Grimm commenced to investigate Indo-European languages, they helped to launch a revival of interest in heroic legend from the North of Europe, out of which came eventually the music dramas of Wagner with their profound effect upon Germanic psychology and the racial doctrines of Nazi Germany in the twentieth century.

It is commonly said that the theories of Sigmund Freud have wrought as great a revolution in our knowledge of human nature as the theories of Charles Darwin wrought in our attitude toward the doctrine of special creation, but Freud himself said that three forces which did most to shape his thought (aside from his technical studies in medicine and neurology) were the Bible, the poetry of Goethe, and *The Origin of Species,* this last being not only a classic of science but a classic of nineteenth-century prose. Ideas are powerful. The results of inquiry may be as incalculable in the humanities as they are in physics or biology, and one would be hard put to it to determine whether the humanist or the scientist or the social scientist has done most to alter civilization.

ELEVEN

How Scholars Are Trained

Young scientists leaving the graduate school may go into teaching, industry, or government work,[1] and in varying proportions so may young social scientists. If we except a few posts in museum work, publishing, and one or two other occupations, young humanists, if they are to follow their professions, look forward to teaching. It cannot be argued that it is more difficult to teach the humanities than it is to teach science or social science, but it can be said that the situation of the humanities is unique and that, because of the concentration of the humanities in university and college, the teaching problem looms large. The means by which the young scholar begins the long course of preparation that will ideally turn him into the man of learning are under constant scrutiny. No pattern satisfies everybody, but the standard pattern includes research training and opportunity for teaching.

The ultimate source of all education in the humanities is, with few exceptions, the graduate school of arts and

[1] Since about 1925 the percentage of scientists in industry has risen from 6 or 7% to something like 45% of Ph.D.'s. Out of a population of some 240,000 scientists, between 110,000 and 115,000 were in industry in 1956. *Expanding Resources of College Teaching*, ed. by Charles G. Dobbins, American Council on Education Studies, Series I, No. 60, Washington, October, 1956, p. 21. About 87% of Ph.D.'s in chemistry leave academic institutions, leaving only a minority to carry on teaching in university and college.

sciences, which, taken department by department, is a professional school, conferring degrees upon historians, chemists, philologists, philosophers, biologists, and so on in the same way and for the same purpose that law schools, medical schools, and divinity schools confer degrees. The two graduate degrees of interest to the humanities are the M.A. and the Ph.D. In the main, a master's degree has become a prerequisite for teaching in the public high schools and the Ph.D. is in fact a prerequisite to a scholar-teacher's career in the academic world.[2] Many schools of education also confer master's degrees, sometimes wholly in professional educational theory, sometimes covering both educational work and "subject matter" courses. A few institutions offer a degree governed jointly by the faculty in arts and sciences and the faculty in education— the Master of Arts in Teaching. The holder of an M.A. only from a graduate school of arts and sciences who wishes to qualify for appointment to a public-school faculty will have to acquire a certain number of credit hours in "education" to do so. There is, then, a variety of M.A.'s that will do for secondary-school work. For a number of reasons, the M.A. is no longer regarded seriously by the academic world as an index of professional attainment, however excellent it may be for pedagogical purposes. The Ph.D. has become in fact the *sine qua non* for a scholar in the United States.[3] It is therefore a matter of moment to know what the degree represents and how it is acquired.

[2] Junior colleges waver between believing an M.A. sufficient to qualify a staff member, and requiring the Ph.D. of staff members.

[3] Equivalents are satisfactory. Thus a Mus.D. (Doctor of Music) is universally regarded as having an equality with the Ph.D. "Lesser" degrees (but they often connote rigorous training) will serve for posts having to do with "practical" courses in some of the fine arts (for example, a B.S. in Arch. or a master's degree in fine arts), but a superior degree is commonly required for higher posts. In appointing an artist, poet, musician, or sculptor as "artist in residence," degree requirements are waived. But so, likewise, are the conventional loads of teaching and conferring with students.

For entrance into the graduate school of arts and sciences the candidate must present evidence that he has acquired a bachelor's degree, together with a transcript of his course work. Except in unusual circumstances he will have to show that he "concentrated" or "majored" in the department of knowledge in which he proposes to pursue graduate work. His record will be scanned to see whether his grades go up or down, whether they represent superior work in his chosen field, and whether he has had any work 1) in the classical languages and in foreign languages and 2) in departments allied to the subject of his choice. But as undergraduate records offer a wide diversity of courses in many fields—for example, in history, English, and Romance languages—and as the divisions among departments are not uniform over the country, it is difficult in the humanities, even when excellence is gauged by a relatively uniform grading system, to be sure that any five candidates for admission to a given field have any preparation in common.[4] The graduate dean, the admitting committee, the chairman of the appropriate department, or whoever undertakes the responsibility does the best he can. Various departments lay down various prescriptions of what they expect of students desiring to do graduate

[4] In the field of English, for example, some departments include work for undergraduates in speech, radio broadcasting, the drama, journalism, creative writing, and other like courses, any and all of which may be counted for an undergraduate "major." Bright undergraduates desiring to enter the graduate school for professional training in the study of English language and literature may, accordingly, lack (a) any historical sense, (b) acquaintance with great familiar classics, (c) any exposure to the study of language in a scientific or scholarly fashion, and (d) any real ability to analyze a text, write competent interpretation, and read aloud acceptably. This is an extreme case, but not so extreme that it never happens. Probably acquaintance with half a dozen Shakespeare plays is all the common knowledge that can be safely counted on over the country from college seniors majoring in English. This, of course, does not mean that they know only Shakespeare. The point lies in the bewildering lack of agreement about what an undergraduate concentration in English is supposed to do.

work under their direction, and these prescriptions will vary in specificity, but they cannot be uniform except verbally. The one prerequisite for advanced work in the humanities likely to be weakest is the requirement of a reading ability in one or more foreign languages or in the classics or in both. The Modern Language Association of America is undertaking an extensive campaign to begin the study of foreign languages earlier in the school system and to see that as a minimum one such language is mastered by the senior year, but the campaign is only just initiated and it has a long way to go.[5]

Having been accepted by some graduate school and having announced his intention to work for a doctorate in some one department of humane learning, the student confronts two general systems of requirements. One, the simpler, is imposed by the graduate school. The second, varying in complexity from department to department, is imposed by the graduate faculty in the specialty of his choice. Theoretically the general pattern of work to be followed is a three-year pattern, though in fact the Ph.D. is seldom acquired within this time limit. In the ideal scheme, the first year of study will be directed toward securing a mastery of the general elements of Romance language and literature, philosophy, fine arts, history, or whatever field is in question. The second year will con-

[5] Some 46% of American high schools offer no course in any foreign language, or at least this was the figure until recently. It is possible to enter and possible to be graduated from liberal arts colleges in some universities without being able to read or speak a foreign language. Minimum requirements for the bachelor's degree in other colleges are of the type of two years of one foreign language and one year of another. The one-year requirement often means beginning a language and then dropping it and the two-year requirement commonly fails to create mastery. These sober considerations make it somewhat difficult to find instructors competent to teach courses in world literature, general literature, comparative literature, or the like, with any facility, although many theorists believe that only by such courses will undergraduates gain a "broad view." Translations are often lacking, frequently perverse, and in any event require from the teacher constant reference to the original text.

centrate upon a particular portion of that field. The third year will be devoted to writing the dissertation. Either at the end of the first year or during the second year, but certainly before the student is permitted to register the subject of his dissertation and begin work on it, he will have to pass a general examination (oral or written or both) administered by his department. Theoretically, at the end of his studies, the dissertation having been written and in most institutions having been accepted by the professor (or committee) in charge, he will have to pass a "final" examination. Only then will he become a doctor of philosophy in a given department of humanistic scholarship.

2

Few students complete their studies in this time or after this ideal pattern, and it is important to understand why degrees are postponed.

So far as the first year is concerned, the student has commonly moved into a new institutional environment, and since the graduate school has its own traditions and way of life, it takes him some time to become adjusted. In the first year of graduate study, moreover, students are commonly expected to prove their ability to read one, two, or three foreign languages, ancient or modern; and since the majority of American students are unable to meet this requirement, some important part of their energies must be devoted to getting up at least a minimum knowledge of these languages. In many cases they do not succeed in passing the required examinations until well into their second year of work.

Because of the variegated nature of undergraduate programs, especially since the coming in of requirements in "general education" which, however meritorious in themselves, do not always give particular mastery of a specific branch of humane learning, many students in the graduate school, in place of using the first year of graduate study to consolidate their mastery of a chosen field, are compelled to drop back into the undergraduate college to take courses in important areas of their subject in which they have had no instruction at all. Inevitably this delays the march into graduate study proper, and sometimes it extends into the second year of graduate work.

Although in theory the doctorate is not awarded for course work but for mastery evidenced to a department through general examination, course work is commonly sought out wherever possible, inasmuch as private reading, though theoretically laudable, is vague. But course work may also delay progress.

Because it is desirable that the future teacher be initiated into the teaching process as soon as possible, commonly during his second year of graduate study the student takes on some form of classwork, either as an assistant (paper reader) to a professor in charge of a large lecture course; or as a part-time tutor; or as a teaching fellow or part-time instructor in charge of a group or section of a large lecture course or of a section in some beginning course, as, for example, freshman composition, introductory philosophy, the first course in the fine arts, and so on. Since, contrary to popular impression, departments in the humanities are enormously interested in ferreting out and encouraging teaching ability, the graduate student is encouraged to take on work of this order. But obviously this delays completing graduate courses. Moreover, the wide spread of courses in general education has meant an increased demand for a junior staff to teach sections of such courses, and this junior staff draws importantly upon graduate students in the humanities.

Since an increasing number of graduate students are married men, sometimes heads of families, responsibility and attention must go to one's domestic life no less than to one's scholarly career; and it is not uncommon for a young father in the graduate school to reduce his work to half time while he earns money to support his family.[6] Sometimes he may drop out of the school for a year or a half-year. All this postpones the completion of the requirements.

At the end of the nineteenth century it was commonly held that a doctoral dissertation must represent a contribution to knowledge in the sense of bringing something undiscovered into the world of learning. Although this concept of the dissertation still lingers, the dissertation is now more commonly regarded (in the humanities, at least) as a test of maturity of mind and of professional competence. It reveals whether the candidate has mastered the tools of his profession and the boundaries and significance of his special field. It is a problem of mature interpretation rather than of originality in the sense of the "unique thing," but it is, and must be, something far richer and fuller, whatever its subject, than a term paper in a course —or, for that matter, three or four such papers. It is, so to say, writing a book under competent direction. But as anybody knows who has ever attempted to do so, writing a book is a chancy thing. Unexpected leads open, unpredictable problems appear, evidence is more scattered than one had assumed, and, finally, the psychology of writing varies significantly from week to week, from chore to chore, and from individual to individual. The consequence is that many dissertations—one suspects, most of them—take longer than their writers had planned for. Putting aside the deliberately dilatory, the "perfectionists," and the incompetent, one finds that dissertations are delayed even

---

[6] An opposite pattern has also become standard. The wife works in order that the husband may study for his degree.

at the hands of irreproachable candidates for the degree.

To complete the work for a doctor's degree will, then, commonly take from four to six years. Every graduate school has its eccentrics, but the fact that there are occasional "tenth-year graduate students" is no indication that in normal cases graduate work is unduly prolonged, given the circumstances that have just been outlined.

The young Ph.D. secures a post in the teaching world upon the recommendation of his professors in the graduate school, usually through the operation of a university appointment bureau. These recommendations almost invariably include three elements: observations upon the personality and promise of the young doctor; observations upon his performance and promise as a scholar; and observations upon his past performance and potentiality as a teacher. The legend has arisen that graduate professors are not interested in the teaching potential of their students. This is contrary to fact.

The pattern of training for the Ph.D. was taken over by American graduate schools from nineteenth-century German universities, which then led the world in scholarly activity. There have been silent modifications of the original Germanic pattern since the founding of Johns Hopkins University in 1876, three of which should be mentioned. 1) The publication of dissertations is no longer a general requirement in the humanities—a necessary and merciful change in the matter of expenses, but a change that has led to the error of supposing the dissertation is no more than a glorified class paper instead of being the ultimate achievement of the graduate student. 2) In American practice in the humanities the dissertation has tended more and more away from being a research contribution to scholarship and more and more in the direction of a mature interpretation of a problem. 3) The preoccupation of nineteenth-century scholars with genetic explanation (on the analogy of biological evolution) has yielded ground to other philosophies of meaning.[7]

3

It is possibly a tribute to the graduate school that doctoral training in the humanities is constantly under criticism or attack.[8] In view of the gap between the theory of humane learning and the inexperience of youth, the apparent discrepancy between the apprentice and the master seems too great. Many demands for alteration of the present system are more emotional than factual, as if there were some mysterious short cut to development the graduate schools were blindly ignoring. Yet even those who would like to alter present patterns agree that scholarly research must continue if the humanities are to remain a dynamic component of American life. All reformers likewise concede that training for scholarship is an essential element of the Ph.D. program. We shall come back to the significance of this unanimity.

Those who are dissatisfied with the existing system are

[7] Literary study is a striking example. As late as 1910 the chief duty of the graduate student was to master the oldest extant forms of the Germanic (or Romance) language system and to study the oldest monuments in a given literature, the theory being that later forms of the language and later literary manifestations would then be easy of comprehension. "Philology" in this sense by and by became an intolerable burden, but with the weakening of the requirement it is also probably true there has come a weakening of the sense of urgency and centrality of comprehending language, in scholarship of all sorts.

[8] Three characteristic pronouncements of recent date are these: 1) *The Graduate School Today and Tomorrow: Reflections for the Profession's Consideration*, written by F. W. Strothmann on behalf of the Committee of Fifteen; published by the Fund for the Advancement of Education, New York, 1955; 2) *Doctoral Studies in English and Preparation for Teaching: A Committee Report of the College English Association*, written for the committee by Alvan S. Ryan, June, 1957; 3) "Report of the Committee on Policies in Graduate Education" presented to the Association of Graduate Schools and available in the New York *Times*, November 13, 1957, p. 28.

not in accord with respect to the changes they desire. Some insist that training for teaching is neglected or minimized. Others complain that getting a Ph.D. "takes too long." A third complaint is that Ph.D. training is "narrow" and needs to be "broadened," sometimes by insisting upon a larger degree of "criticism" or of "interpretation," and sometimes by asking for more immediate awareness of current problems. A fourth group would abolish the dissertation, a fifth would substitute for it a group of three or four long papers, and a sixth would alter its character in the direction of "critical interpretation." Finally, objections are raised to the foreign-language requirements, and this is sometimes coupled with a demand that the candidate's command of English be improved.

Better English is always desirable, and undoubtedly many dissertations are dully written. There are, however, two confusions here. The young scholar is talking professionally to other scholars, not to the general public, and the dissertation, usually the first formal act of scholarship by the student, is directed at an audience of experts, not to readers of the *Atlantic Monthly*. Style follows function and form, not the reverse. In the second place, the term "better English" is seldom or never defined and as the criteria by which improvement is to be measured are never made clear, this reform comes down to the general proposition that all adults should be encouraged to write and speak with greater elegance, precision, and force, a proposition that can scarcely be contested.

Those who would abolish the present foreign-language requirements present several arguments. They point to science—for example, to chemistry—and say that scientists find that English abstracts of papers and dissertations in a foreign tongue are quite usable.[9] They argue with con-

[9] Useful they are, and there seems to be no reason why the humanities should not employ the method of abstracts in English more regularly

siderable justice that the requirement is inefficient, since students cannot read the languages even after they have passed the canonical reading examinations in them. Finally, they infer that if the same amount of time and energy were spent in wider reading and more writing, humanistic scholarship would improve.

Arguments for abolishing the requirement fly in the face of the program of the Modern Language Association for improving the teaching of foreign languages; and the argument that scholarship will improve by stripping itself of a mode of communication with other cultures was contradicted practically by the American government when it created the Foreign Service Institute to teach languages to Americans sent abroad on official service. The interest in "communication" among philosophers, philologists, teachers of writing, businessmen, and engineers, moreover, would seem to demand a wider rather than a lesser experience with language. American scholars can scarcely expect all foreign scholars to learn English while the Americans learn no foreign languages at all. Finally, the cry to broaden the Ph.D. commonly means that the young scholar is to learn more about other cultures, but how cutting him off from foreign languages will assist him in this respect does not appear. The present foreign-language requirements are inefficient, but that there should be none at all does not follow. In a universe in which Russian, Chinese, Moslem, Hispanic, and Indic cultures loom large amid the crash of European empires, it would seem ill-advised to declare that American humanists need know only English. If young scholars here, unlike young scholars everywhere else in the world, cannot learn two lan-

than they do. The monthly *Abstracts of English Studies* was founded in 1958 with this purpose in view in the fields of English and American literary history. But in the "tight case" the scientist or the scholar wants to get back to the *ipsissima verba* of the foreign specialist. This is precisely the reason for the foreign-language requirement.

guages other than their own, let them learn one, at least, thoroughly, and let departments re-examine their rules and the meaning of their rules.

Those who attack the dissertation or who would substitute some other exercise for it commonly do so because they think graduate training "takes too long" and is "narrowing." Many students, they argue, do not become productive scholars—why, then, the universal requirement of a research degree and a dissertation? There is force in these observations. But those who make them also agree that humanistic research is essential to the life of humane learning. Inevitably, therefore, reformers face a dilemma they have not yet resolved: either one graduate program or two; either one degree or a pair. But if there are two programs or two degrees, one primarily for the research scholar and one for the teacher, then the concept of the teacher-scholar who develops into the man of learning disappears. How are the two programs to be kept in such balance that prestige will attach itself equally to both? Either the Ph.D. with its long tradition and solid core will pale its ineffectual fire before a new degree, or the new degree will become inferior and descend to the level of the present M.A., which was once a scholar's degree and has now lost significance in research scholarship.[10] Thus far, at any rate, no university has seriously considered some other sort of degree in the humanities.[11] Nor is this necessarily stubbornness; it may be only a wise caution.

[10] The ambiguous status of the M.A. is further increased by the practice in many departments of making it a terminal degree for misfits who have tried the Ph.D. and failed. In such cases the department will award the M.A. as a kind of consolation prize or apology for the department's original error in admitting the candidate to graduate work, and simultaneously forbid him to go on to the Ph.D.

[11] In *Education and World Tragedy*, Harvard University Press, 1948, the writer proposed the creation of a Graduate School for administering one degree and a Graduate College for administering the other, but the suggestion has not been taken up.

Those who regard the dissertation as a bed of Procrustes on which individuality is sacrificed to conformity do not admit that a new wind is blowing through the graduate world and do not understand that the chief importance of the dissertation is to the young scholar, not to the general public. He may, of course, discover an important uncollected text or be able to identify a hitherto unidentified monastery in North Africa, and if he does so he contributes new facts to knowledge. But this is not the whole story about dissertations. In writing the dissertation the young scholar is for the first time in his life left alone in library or museum to produce a book-length study, a far more responsible undertaking than writing a term paper or even two or three of them. He confronts some sort of relatively major problem, one he has consented to try to solve. Here is the library, the museum, the record office, there stands the graduate professor ready to advise but by no means the tyrant of humorous fancy, and far on the horizon shine all sorts of fascinating possibilities in the way of evidence—private papers in somebody's garret, a special collection of documents in such and such a library, somebody's dissertation in Rome or Frankfurt, a bronze in a Stockholm museum, reports of archaeological finds in Crete, an interview with a living philosopher.[12] He enters upon the world of learning no longer in pupillary garb but as a citizen of an intellectual empire. For one dissertation the student may do no more than read systematically the works of an author from a particular point of view. For another he patiently studies the proof revisions of a great poet to see how an artist refines his style. For a third he may inquire into the operation of some general concept in the history of ideas. For a fourth he recovers and re-

---

[12] Read in this connection the prefatory matter by Christopher Morley and Frederick A. Pottle to *Boswell's London Journal*, in The New American Library, 1956.

vivifies musical compositions dead these many years and now brought back to life by sympathy and learning. Another dissertation shows, perhaps, how a historian read a forgotten book, as Jules Michelet read Giovanni Vico, and how it transformed his view of the world. Or he may trace the fortune of a word or phrase across the centuries, of some decorative design from country to country, of a key idea from one philosopher to another, of a musical form from church to church. It is on the whole fair to say that no substitute for this immensely beneficial exercise has yet been devised. No mere "paper" can induce the same enriching sense of the thrill of discovery, the private voyaging on strange seas of thought alone, the tedious toil by which books—even bad books—get themselves put together, the difference between authoritative knowing and slapdash guessing. Writing a dissertation, that stale subject for jesting, can be, and in most cases is, a valuable exercise in the pedagogy of learning, and it is difficult to see what can be substituted for it.

The Germanic Ph.D. paid no attention to teacher training for the simple reason that it assumed that the program and the dissertation were an introduction to learning, to membership in the society of scholars. Increasingly, however, beneficial pressures on the American university have compelled the graduate school to face the fact that most Ph.D.'s in the humanities will teach. We have glanced at some of the more customary methods of introducing the future professor to classroom work. Other schemes have been and are being devised. One such is an "internship" program, wherein the young scholar takes up teaching as a temporary member of a college department and participates not only in teaching but also in seminar discussions of teaching. Another scheme—the Vanderbilt program—adds two courses in the usual Ph.D. requirement, one in the make-up of the American college, a second in "Basic

Ideas," and, in addition, provides for supervised teaching. In other institutions beginning instructors are assigned to veteran members of a department for supervision, consolation, and advice. Seven liberal arts colleges in Southern California have combined to administer a joint program for young scholar-teachers which includes inter-subject seminars and fortnightly discussions of topics relevant to college teaching. All this is to the good.

There are, of course, difficulties. A given graduate department may properly attract more graduate students than it can possibly offer part-time teaching posts. The cost of additional instruction in teaching, moreover, has to be borne by somebody, and although foundations have been generous in financing such programs, they cannot pay for everything. There is also sometimes generated an attitude toward some required courses and toward the dissertation that is regrettable, as if these were unaccountable and irrational obstacles in place of being adjuncts to the teaching problem. Principally, however, the great difficulty is that as the circle of apprentice teachers grows, students and alumni increasingly complain that they came or sent their children to college to be taught by the "big men," not as guinea pigs for pedagogical experimentation by learners. The assumption that the "big man" is a veteran teacher and the beginner a mere botcher is not quite true, since the beginner brings a freshness, enthusiasm, and sense of responsibility to the classroom the veteran may not exhibit, but keeping a nice balance between instruction by the professorial faculty and practice teaching by the young is a delicate problem in administration and finance. On the whole, however, the concern of graduate schools for teaching has honorably increased in all branches of knowledge and not least in the humanities.

Finally, there are the associated charges that the Ph.D. needs to be made "broad" and that it "takes too long," but these are baffling statements. How long is too long? How broad is broad? It is admitted on all sides that knowledge of all kinds has tremendously increased in the twentieth century. Is this knowledge, or some part of it, to be somehow thoroughly mastered in less time than it took to master less knowledge? Or do we not want masterly humanists? So far as thoroughness goes, if the humanities are to gain respect among thoughtful students, they who profess them cannot be second-rate, ill-disciplined minds compared with first-rate, thoroughly disciplined minds in science and social science. Art is at least as exacting and subtle as physics; history demands, though in different form, as much patience, knowledge, and skill as economics. One will not gain anything for the humanities by facile teaching or shallow study. As for "broad," it is commonly companioned with "narrow" and mistaken for "broadening." Specialization—that is, the mastery of something—is occasionally narrow and even narrowing, but it is quite as often—nay, more often—thorough and deep. A great scholar, by his very existence, broadens us because he compels us to discipline our vague and sentimental generalities. Scrutinizing with loving care the text of Dante may be even more enriching—and therefore broadening—than a sweeping course in Western Civilization. Americans respect the Man Who Knows, not one who keeps his few valid ideas in the store window of his personality.

If, however, what is meant—and this has point—is that specialization in the Western humanities, and in them only, is a kind of cultural parochialism the country can ill afford, this sort of broadening is going to take more time, not less, competence in more languages rather than in fewer, more abundant knowledge, not sparser information, and books, dissertations, and articles consuming a greater amount of energy, not a lesser degree of it. In no conceivable circumstances can the degree program be shortened or become more superficial if this is the intent of training. Faulty the American Ph.D. system is, but this is no reason for throwing the baby out with the bath. The world respects American scientists and social scientists; it will not come to respect either American scholarship or American culture if those who speak for the humanities are in any way less thoroughly educated than those in the other two great areas of thought. Mastery of his subject, maturity of judgment, and the capacity to create lasting work in critical and scholarly interpretation of art and thought—these are still the world's aim in humanistic learning, as they must be the aim of citizens of the United States concerned for higher education.

4

There are deeper and more vexatious problems in finding proper teachers of humane learning. To these we must briefly turn, but it must be understood that the following observations are as nearly objective as they can be made. Humanists achieve nothing by complaints that they are not understood, not wanted, or not supported, nor is anything gained by picturing science and the social sciences as enemies. Knowledge is a single whole.

1. At both ends of the educational spectrum the sciences enjoy advantages natural to a technological culture that the humanities cannot possess. These advantages have been increased in the post-Sputnik era with its emotional demands for more science and more scientists, but they are not merely the product of current fears.

In the first place, it is possible to identify potential scientific talent much earlier than it seems possible to identify potential humanistic talent. Much attention (though in the opinion of many scientists not enough) has therefore been given to discovering and encouraging young scientists in the secondary schools through such organizations as Science Talent Search and such annual events as Science Fairs. Moreover, industry commonly offers more scholarship aid to science-minded undergraduates than it does to undergraduates in the humanities; and seniors in science have opportunities for better-paid jobs than do students specializing in the humanities, whose job opportunities are commonly confined to teaching.

In the second place, because of the growing habit among industrialists of turning research problems over to graduate schools or like parts of the university and of paying for the working out of the problem, graduate professors in the sciences (or the graduate dean) have opportunities to finance science students working for the Ph.D. that are denied graduate students in the humanities. This opportunity is increased by government grants through the National Science Foundation. Thus in 1956–57 this foundation awarded 855 predoctoral fellowships in the natural sciences and allied fields, and eighty postdoctoral fellowships. First-year fellowships carried stipends of $1,400; intermediate fellowships carried stipends of $1,600, and terminal-year fellowships stipends of $1,800. Postdoctoral fellowships were worth $3,400. "Allied fields" included the social sciences, but not the humanities. The humanities as such cannot parallel this munificence. Today (1958) federal legislation greatly increases the total monetary rewards available for studying science.

2. It is possible, though with less certainty than in the case of science, to identify adolescent artistic talent in the secondary schools, but impossible to prophesy that the art-minded high-school pupil is going to submit to the long and grueling discipline which alone guarantees first-class achievement in the fine arts. Because of popular confusion of the fine arts with humanistic scholarship, the failure of the young artist so to develop even when he or she has

had a well-meant subsidy has sometimes been translated into either an indictment of the humanities or the belief that since talent in art is so unpredictable, you had better not risk money on it. But even if the encouragement of potential artists identifiable in high school were uniformly productive of lasting results, it does not follow that humane learning would profit. Talent for scholarship is not the same thing as talent for painting, dancing, music, writing, or acting. The discipline of the artist is not identical with the discipline of the scholar, and in fact the humanities have not benefited from this variety of educational aid, which is seldom extended to a pupil merely proficient in Latin, or history, or the study of the literary classics. Such pupils have commonly to depend upon a vague general trust in scholarship.

3. Another problem, the mere statement of which arouses controversy, arises out of the empirical fact that in general humanists tend to mature professionally later than do scientists. Inasmuch as ripening among humanists is supposed to be in the direction of philosophy and wisdom, scientists, rightly believing that philosophy and wisdom are no monopoly of the humanities, incline to bristle at what seems to be the implication of the empiric truth. It is not here contended that able scientists lack philosophy or wisdom or that aging humanists necessarily possess both. Yet the observable gap between the sagacious and experienced man of learning and an eager, bright, intelligent, yet one-sided and inexperienced Ph.D. starting his career in the humanities is more evident, on the whole, than is the gap between the brilliant young chemist, physicist, biologist, or other specialist in natural or physical science and established figures in his department. The truth of the observation is re-enforced in the complaint of parents that their offspring, enrolled in courses in English, history, philosophy, or whatnot, are taught by beginners,

whereas complaint is not vehemently raised at a like condition in laboratory courses in science. Research scientists, it is alleged, reach their apogee in the mid- or later thirties or the early forties, whereas in the humanities this condition is more common in the late forties or the fifties. In consequence, the young scholar in the humanities sometimes looks greener by comparison with elder statesmen in *his* field than does the young scientist in his department. Criticism follows; and on the campus, in student reports or the college newspaper, humanities departments may suffer from a bad press.

4. Finally, there is the flattering expectation that the humanist is somehow supposed to "pull things together," an obligation from which, apparently, the scientist in educational discussion is released. He who reads articles about teaching in the humanities ceases by and by to be amazed at pronouncements as sweeping as these:

The humanities "show the real unity of mankind."

The humanities "are what make a civilization civilized rather than barbarous."

"Man has lost faith in man," there is needed "a new message of hope and faith," and "this is the call which American humanists must answer."

"It is the humanist who sits in judgment on the importance of the use to which scientific knowledge is put."

"The dilution of the solid core of education in the humanities has transferred responsibility and burden from the discipline to the instructor."

"Scholarship is simply the unceasing effort to bring order into the confusion of tradition."

"The humanities deal with ideas . . . it is through education that diseased ideas must be replaced by sound ideas, that the will for good must be implanted . . .

that knowledge essential to wise action must be com-
municated . . . and that understanding of beauty
and power of self-expression must be nurtured." [13]

Any one of these statements may be impeccable and philosophic; taken together, they impose a frightening prospect
upon the young teacher, who is also told that: "In philosophy the sheer intellectual labor of grappling with certain
ideas or trains of thought has often obscured the purpose
of grasping them" and that "Judgments of value are not
judgments of correctness or conformity; they are judgments of effect and of utility. One does not know the effect
or the utility until he knows something of the end product." [14] Instructed that ignorance of the ways of other
peoples causes war and that "to dispel this ignorance and
to replace it by understanding is a social obligation of
American humanistic scholars of the greatest urgency";
instructed also that "it is for the scholars in the humanities
to comprehend the vast scope and also the intricate detail
of American studies," without forgetting "the importance
for the humanities of close relations with other disciplines," [15] reminded by the president of one great scholarly
organization that "The mastery of foreign tongues, ancient
and modern, the sciences of epigraphy and palaeography

[13] These statements and others like them may be found in: Monroe E.
Deutsch, "The Foes of the Humanities," *Proceedings of the Western College Association,* 1952–53, p. 48; George Boas, "The Humanities and Defense," *Journal of Higher Education,* XXII, May 1, 1951, p. 232; Hayward
Keniston, "Champions of the Great Tradition," *PMLA,* 69, March, 1954,
p. 8; Abraham Flexner as quoted in I. L. Kandel, "The Future of the
Humanities," *School and Society,* 75, May 24, 1952, p. 332; Lawrence C.
Lockley, "Business Education and the Humanities," *School and Society,*
74, December 29, 1951, p. 30; Jacques Barzun, "The Scholar Is an Institution," *Journal of Higher Education,* XVIII, November, 1947, pp. 393–394;
Waldo G. Leland, "The Present Task of the Humanities," *School and
Society,* 64, October 26, 1946, pp. 282, 283.
[14] Joseph J. Firebaugh, "Freedom and the Humanities," *The Educational Forum,* 17, 1953, p. 458.
[15] Leland, *op. cit.,* pp. 283, 284.

for the deciphering of old monuments, textual criticism, the study and interpretation of authors, the patient assembling of data in history and biography . . . will always be essential elements in sound scholarship and scholarship will not remain sound unless the training in such disciplines is fairly widespread," [16] and by the head of another that "We must make the past more vivid and the quality of man's adventure more deeply understood; we must interpret the past broadly, in the spirit of a man to whom nothing human is alien; we need not be afraid to speak of moral values, to be sensitive and compassionate, or to exalt wisdom and goodness; we must set the example of a sound intellectual and moral balance, of a broad view of human values; we must make the processes of the mind in seeking truth so far, so understanding of various opinions, and yet so clear that they will command respect and deserve imitation," [17] the young scholar-teacher may be pardoned if he feels embarrassed or crushed by the weight of the professional obligations laid upon him, discouraged by the impossibility of fulfilling a tithe of these tremendous chores, and embittered in some degree by the doctrine that graduate work in science is so difficult and necessary it has to be paid for by government and industry, whereas graduate work in the humanities—those disciplines which "sit in judgment on the importance of the use to which scientific knowledge is put"—drags its heels, a poor third in the race for proper support in a democratic culture that began as a system of general philosophic ideas and is still supposed to be nourished by their spread among our citizens.

[16] Fred Norris Robinson, "Retrospect and Prospect," *PMLA*, 60, Supplement, 1945, pp. 1292–1305. "Let us," the passage concludes, "be loyal to the established standards of the humanities."

[17] Dexter Perkins, "We Shall Gladly Teach," *The American Historical Review*, LXII, January, 1957, pp. 291–309, the presidential address at the 1956 meeting.

Epilogue

TWELVE

Needs

How can the ordinary citizen help the humanities?
In order to understand the magnitude and variety of
the tasks the humanities have had to assume in American
education, let us begin by listing their more important
responsibilities.

1. Persons professionally interested in the humanities
are supposed to teach the rudiments of our own language
and the rudiments of foreign languages, ancient and modern, including the Oriental tongues, to American youth.

2. They are supposed to teach American youth the
rudiments of philosophy, ethics, logic, aesthetics (or at
least taste), and, in some cases, the bases of religious faith.

3. They are supposed to inculcate in pupil or student
a competent style in speaking and writing, including
pupils or students temperamentally averse to polite learning (indeed, precisely because they are averse!).

4. They are supposed to inculcate and encourage habits of reading which shall be lifelong. "Reading" means
not only mere literacy and the habit of reading good books
(*i.e.*, better current fiction), but also an abiding taste for
"serious" reading, that is, for books in literature, history,
philosophy, and so forth that have established worth and
that carry greater intellectual weight than is commonly
found in the contemporary output of print.

5. Along with the teaching of languages professional humanists are supposed to create through, or at any rate along with, this teaching a comprehension of the culture, history, social psychology, and needs of the people or peoples speaking, reading, or writing the language or languages studied; or, in the case of the "dead" languages, the people or peoples who spoke, read, and wrote them.

6. They are also supposed to create and encourage a lifelong taste for the fine arts, music, the theater, literature, good architecture, the dance as an art form, excellent decoration, and so forth, or for one or some of these; and though every student is not supposed to be equally skilled in or sympathetic with all the arts in question, he is supposed through humane learning to discover that these arts exist, why they exist, and what great names, structures, paintings, and so on are associated with them for every cultivated person to know.

7. These same specialists are supposed to discover, create, encourage, or sustain in students something like the theory and practice of criticism (or rational judgment upon performances in the arts, or, for that matter, performance in philosophy and related subjects); and in fulfilling this task, the specialists are expected to be equally sympathetic with past masterpieces and with present attempts to vie with them.

8. They are also expected to make students mildly conversant, at least, with the cultural development of the Western world, and increasingly they are expected to know, sympathize with, and teach a) something about the cultural outlooks of the Orient and b) something of a "world view" of religions, faiths, cultures, and philosophies.

9. Along with this "world-view" approach these same scholar-teachers are expected to create in their students a capacity for an ethical outlook upon life.

10. They are supposed to examine sympathetically the ideational basis of "Western democratic traditions" and in so doing also make "better citizens" out of American youth.

11. They are supposed to discover and encourage "creativity."

12. Their teaching is supposed to guide young people to a "sane emotional balance." This implies something called individual growth in appreciation and knowledge (understanding).

13. They are expected to interpret on a nontechnical basis the general humane, philosophic, or metaphysical significance for "modern man" of modern science and modern social science no less than modern art.

14. Persons professionally skilled in humane learning are supposed through appropriate pedagogical devices and skillful teaching to offset the allegedly narrowing influence upon youth of too much or too intense technical (technological) education in science, engineering, business, and other professional curriculums or schools which call in the humanities principally for this therapeutic purpose.

15. Through the instrumentality of graduate work humanistic scholars are expected not only to train the young specialist in scholarly techniques, the history and substance of his chosen specialty, and modes of explicating it, but also to make teaching an attractive pursuit to the humanistic neophyte.

16. Humanistic scholars are expected to carry on original research and to write it up. If they do not do so, their chances of professional advancement steadily lessen. What they find out, they are expected to publish, in particular instances, if necessary, finding or supplying the funds to do this.

17. Humanistic scholarship is supposed to furnish a

constant flow of fresh and accurate information to the general public.

18. Specialists in the humanities are, of course, expected to be masters of some specialty in their general area of humane learning, to know the general field with which they are associated as well, and to read books and articles by specialists in that field, and, so far as they can, to keep up with books "outside" their specialties because such books are books "every educated person ought to know."

19. Scholars in the humanities are expected to serve when called upon as editors of learned journals, or as consulting editors, or as professional readers for such journals. Not infrequently they serve on the board of editorial control of a university press, or for a textbook house, or for a general publisher, or for such general and intelligent magazines as the *American Scholar*. They also serve on committees of specialists for learned societies, or for the American Council of Learned Societies, or on committees of selection for awards, prizes, fellowships, and honors. For this service they commonly receive no extra compensation. They are not unique in having tasks like this to perform, yet such tasks are added professional responsibilities the humanist cannot dodge, even if he wanted to. Compensation for work of this kind is less common in the humanities than in any other field of scholarly activity except the divinity school.

20. Academic departments of the humanities are jointly responsible with schools or departments of education for "training teachers" for the public high schools; and they are wholly or mainly responsible for educating future members of the staffs of private preparatory schools. In many state universities members of a department in the humanities may be assigned to become liaison officers with the school of education or with representatives of the state school system. In any event, humane learning and hu-

manistic scholarship are expected to give sympathy and support to humane teaching in secondary education.

2

Here, then, are twenty central responsibilities undertaken by the humanities, humane learning, and humanistic scholarship. The list (except for item 20) does not separate higher learning from the responsibilities of secondary education. The reason is obvious. Colleges and universities regularly maintain elementary instruction in English, the foreign languages, the classical tongues, and the ability to read,[1] just as they have had to maintain introductory courses in mathematics and science. An important fraction of the energies of humanistic scholars is, therefore, of necessity devoted to elementary instruction. This, together with their other major responsibilities, gives the humanities an impossible work load. They do not have the man power, the money, or the equipment to do the task as it should be done. They do the best they can.

How can the layman help?

1. In the first place he can try to understand the humanities, humane learning, and humanistic scholarship. Professors of English do not confine their professional lives to the study of the comma, nor to teaching girls and boys how to write, speak, and read, and it is as much a mistake to think about the work of the humanities in terms like these as it would be to think about physics in terms of plumbing, or economics in terms of double-entry bookkeeping. Scholarship is wider. It is a normal, rational human activity, and has been honored as such since the days

[1] Courses in "remedial reading" are becoming commonplace in American colleges and universities. The necessity for simple instruction in how to get meaning from a printed page is as widespread as the necessity for simple instruction in the writing of simple English. In many institutions Freshman English is, among other matters, an unavowed course in remedial reading.

of ancient Egypt. You do not dismiss the problem by saying that the scholar is absent-minded, impractical, bookish,
or various other things. Impracticality, if it exists, is no
more a function of scholarship than it is of business, the
law, or medicine; it is a function of personality, not of
professional training, and professional training, though it
may occasionally modify, cannot create or control personal
endowment. Yet until we get rid of the comic-strip notion
of scholarship, we cannot restore proper balance to education and to the national culture. Anybody who seriously
thinks he has disposed of scholarship by charging that
Professor X "never met a payroll" ought to spend a week
in the household of an assistant professor of Romance
languages with a wife, one child, another coming, and
no certainty about promotion—he will learn how to make
both ends meet in a way he will never learn from a directors' meeting.

Scholarship is a profession. In this it resembles law,
medicine, museum work, acting, personnel management,
the ministry, and many other vocations. Its point of view
is as essential to the total national picture as is the point
of view of any other profession from that of war to that
of the ministry. To infer or assume, as some have done,
that scholarship is an escape from reality into a sort of
never-never land is an inexcusable error. Scholarship is not
an escape from reality; it is part of reality, it *is* reality,
since, if there were no scholarship, it would be hard to
think of us as a nation. There would be no art museums,
libraries, theaters, parks, household decorations, or holi-
days, just as there would be no formal religion, no laws,
and no courts. Without scholarship there is no history,
and no tradition, and no notion of the meaning of
words like "justice," "right," "fair practice," "contract,"
"beauty," "the Christian tradition," "authority," "liberty," or "the United States."

2. The ordinary citizen can address himself to the present imbalance between the support given science in the United States and the support given the humanities. This imbalance, which is not the creation of reputable scientists, has been increased, no doubt, by popular fears engendered in the post-Sputnik era and by varying political maneuvers, none of which need hinder anybody from inquiring what proportion of a nation's income should be spent on scientific work profitable to industry or necessary to government, and what proportion should be spent on values that are conceivably more intangible but that are also conceivably quite as important in maintaining the republic.

We spend an enormous amount of money on science, the teaching of science (and technology), and scientific research, though only a small fraction of what is spent goes to the support of basic research. We spend less on the social sciences, and still less on the humanities. Some of the figures, not generally known, are rather astounding. For example, a careful report published in 1951 estimated that the financial aid per capita for original research in the sciences was about $1,800 a year, in the social sciences, $600, and in the humanities $130. The report gravely comments: "The relative positions of the three fields will surprise no one who is familiar with the academic scene." [2] A society that, as between the scientist and the humanist,

[2] Elbridge Sibley, *Support for Independent Scholarship and Research: A Study Supported by the American Philosophical Society and the Social Science Research Council,* New York, 1951, p. 58. The specific figures have been disputed, and it has been argued, among other things, that the high figure for science is fallacious, inasmuch as the cost of materials for scientific research is higher than that for research in other fields. But the problem is not what the money is spent for so much as it is what proportions of the national income go to the three great divisions of research work, and there is reason to suppose that the discrepancy between the amount spent by the scientist and that spent by the humanistic scholar has increased since the report was published. In virtually every important table in the Sibley report the humanistic scholar comes out third.

values the former over the latter in the proportion of
something like fourteen to one is, if the history of mankind be any evidence, not a healthy society. But the trend
continues.

For example, when the National Science Foundation
was created in 1950–51, the year of the Sibley report, it
was given a budget of $225,000. The National Science
Foundation is one of the principal arms of government
for encouraging the teaching of science. In 1958 the president's budget message recommended for this organization
an appropriation of $140 millions, an amount about 600
times the original appropriation, $82 millions of which
were to be spent in the training (or teaching) of scientists
and of science teachers. The so-called "education" budget
message of 1958, which followed on the heels of the first
one, recommended that the teaching of foreign languages
be encouraged (and paid for, if need be) in the interests of
national defense—scarcely a humanistic ideal, however
praiseworthy in itself—but, this aside, the existence of
humanistic scholarship was not recognized. Again: in 1956
the president created a "National Committee for the Development of Scientists and Engineers," but there is no
similar national committee for the development of the
humanities, humane learning, and humanistic scholarship.
The Sixth Annual Report of the National Science Foundation has in it some striking passages. For example:

Down to 1955, the roughly estimated total expenditure for
scientific research and development in the United States was
about $3 billion to $3.5 billion. Based on statements from
10,000 business enterprises and on estimates of costs of research conducted by educational institutions, Government
agencies, and other types of research organizations . . .
United States expenditures for all research and development
for the survey period 1953, were not $3.5 billion but well over
$5 billion . . . private industry alone expended $3.7 billion,

of which $1.4 billion (37%) represented work done for the Federal Government.

The report goes on to say that twenty of the fifty-six departments and agencies of the federal government "administer funds for scientific research and development." [3] What are the parallel figures for the humanities? There are none. We do not know. The federal government does not attempt to collect such statistics in that field, the task of collecting them is too great for the American Council of Learned Societies, and no foundation has as yet undertaken to find out. The annual budget of the American Council of Learned Societies is about half a million in good years, or 1/280 of that proposed for the National Science Foundation in 1958. The endowment of the ACLS is now (April, 1958) $65,000. That of the Social Science Research Council is a little more than $3 million. The National Research Council (the equivalent body for the sciences, not to be confused with the National Science Foundation) does not have to worry about endowment, since it is supported by the United States Government. Federal agencies attempt to identify and classify all the varieties of scientific talent in the country; a similar attempt by the American Council of Learned Societies was cut off untimely some years ago by refusal of funds, so that we literally do not know what specialists in the humanities are available to us in the United States today, or how many of them there are. The federal government directly appropriates nothing for humanistic scholarship, whatever it may do indirectly by maintaining the Library of Congress, the National Gallery, and other useful institutions, just as indirectly it benefits all scholarship and all research through the Fulbright program, the Smith-Mundt act, and other legislation, but we can not judge how great is the

[3] National Science Foundation, *Sixth Annual Report for the Fiscal Year ended June 30, 1956,* Washington, D. C., pp. 1–8.

disparity between what we do governmentally (or, for that matter, institutionally) for the sciences and what we do for the humanities; all that we know is that the disparity seems to be vastly disproportionate to enduring values and to the national needs.[4]

The disproportion is great, it seems to be increasing, and it is not good for the humanities, for the social sciences, for science, or for the nation.

3. The ordinary citizen can exert his influence to see that a larger fraction of the money given to colleges, universities, libraries, museums, research institutions, and the like goes for the general purposes of humane learning or for specific purposes in humanistic scholarship, and not for something else. It is easy for the automotive industry to give funds to engineering schools, for companies manufacturing synthetics, fertilizers, or the like to endow graduate work in chemistry, for great corporations to interest themselves in colleges of business administration, for newspaper wealth to set up such admirable institutions as the Nieman Fellowships in Journalism, for philanthropists to give money to medical research, and so on. It requires, apparently, a higher degree of imaginative faith to invest in the invisible and the intangible. Yet humane learning, essentially invisible and intangible, is central to a good life, a good nation, and a good culture—only, we take it

[4] One major difficulty in estimating the support or lack of it for humanistic scholarship in American institutions is that support for the humanities is often tangled with the general budget of the college of liberal arts; or harassed administrators point to the cost of maintaining a library as proof of their interest in the humanities. But the budget of a college of liberal arts is obviously an over-all budget for the sciences, the social sciences, the humanities, and other activities (for example, the department of physical education), and a library is not used by humanists only, but by all departments of a given faculty, if in varying degrees. So, likewise, the administrator may claim he is supporting humanistic scholarship by supporting a university press, and this is to a limited degree true. But it is also to a limited degree true that he is supporting the social sciences and science as well, since all members of the faculty (or of any faculty) are potential authors of university press books.

for granted. There are no large corporations selling philosophical values, manufacturing aesthetic or moral insight, or piling up profits in archaeology, history, poetry, or music for string quartets. The line of obvious interest which runs from the business world to certain parts of the university and the graduate schools simply does not exist in the realm of the humanities. Nobody subsidizes Plato, although everybody exclaims that of course he would be glad to help him if he could but identify him—in this case, the Plato of the future. We need men of large vision, men who are convinced that without vision the people perish, the nation weakens. We need as a nation an abiding sense of the slow and painful way by which modern man got to where he precariously is. *It is this fundamental sense basic to the humanities that needs to be subsidized before it grows weaker even than it is today.*

3

What is money needed for?

1. *Fellowships.* We do not know the exact amount of fellowship money now available to students and teachers of the humanities in the United States, but it is empirically a cold and sober truth that this amount needs to be increased at least by a factor of ten if the humanities, humane learning, and humanistic scholarship are to keep up with the present subsidies available to science and other branches of knowledge. Existing fellowship funds are utterly inadequate. The number of fellowships available to humanistic scholars is inadequate. The stipend available for existing fellowships, whether for students or for faculty members, is in nine cases out of ten inadequate—inadequate for living during the time covered by the grant, inadequate for traveling expenses, inadequate for the preparation of a manuscript, inadequate for getting

the manuscript published. *There is not a college or a university in the United States which could not benefit from the gift of fellowship funds for mature work in the humanities.* If gifts are not to be made to particular academic institutions, gifts should be made to some central body in the humanities like the American Council of Learned Societies. In 1957 this body had $100,000 for fellowships. The highest amount that could be awarded an individual was $7,000. It received about 575 applications; and a seasoned selection committee, the members of which had had long experience in awarding Fulbright fellowships and other grants, virtually threw up its hands. Somewhere between eighty and a hundred of the applications were top-flight, but it could give only a small fraction of these what they asked for and then its money was exhausted. At this rate it would take five or six years to grant proper fellowships to the Class A applicants of 1957 alone, but in the meantime more applications will be coming in an ever-increasing volume.[5]

2. *General Gifts.* If we take the American Council of Learned Societies, which now comprises twenty-nine national organizations dedicated to humanistic scholarship (including prominent organizations in the social sciences), as representative, we can see the desperate need of money for the furtherance of humanistic scholarship. The endowment fund of the American Council of Learned Societies is about $65,000. Its annual budget (made possible by gifts from various foundations) is about $500,000. These amounts are mere postage-stamp money in comparison with what is anually spent on research in other areas. The American Council of Learned Societies ought to be in a position to spend at least $5 million annually for the

[5] The Ford Foundation and the Carnegie Corporation jointly granted similar amounts for two parallel programs, one for grants-in-aid and one for prizes to be given outstanding scholars, but despite this generosity the fellowship situation remains as stated in the text.

furtherance of research and teaching in the humanities—
an amount which would then be only 1/28 of the funds
proposed for the National Science Foundation in 1958. It
ought to have an endowment fund, not of $65,000, but of
$10 million in order to insure its permanent life, its
permanent staff, and permanent and proper facilities. We
think too meanly of the humanities in this country.

3. *Publication.* The problem haunting humanistic
scholarship is the problem of publication. The costs of
manufacturing and publishing books in this country, during the past half century, have increased by about 600%
if sober estimates are to be believed. It is no longer possible, in these days of mass media, for the general publisher, however well disposed toward serious reading, to
bring out important books for a relatively small public.
Very few manuscripts by scholars are now accepted by
general publishing houses. The scholar can, of course, turn
to the textbook publisher, but the textbook publisher is
also inevitably interested in mass sales if he can get them;
consequently he has to cater to the lowest common denominator of demand as reported to him by his salesmen,
and not to the results of research in the humanities. Moreover, a textbook is not the same thing as scholarship. If
the scholar turns to the university presses, he is somewhat
better off, but the university presses likewise have to pay
increased costs for the manufacturing and sale of books;
and though their situation has been somewhat alleviated
by grants from foundation sources, they are again and
again compelled to ask the scholar, or his friends, or the
institution to which he belongs, or the learned association
of which he is a member, to furnish some sort of subsidy
for his book, fruit of a long period of research activity.
Nothing is more heartbreaking than the disappearance
from the academic world of the "monograph series" possible in earlier times, in which the results of serious in-

vestigation by humanistic scholars could be presented to the world of scholarship. If these have not totally vanished from the American scene, they are dwindling in number. So, likewise, the financial support of many scholarly journals is precarious; and whereas in many European countries scholars are paid for their contributions to such periodicals, they are not paid in this country, where virtually every learned journal needs increased financial support.

4. *Conference and Meetings.* Research scientists and social scientists enjoy wonderful professional opportunities for professional intercourse. All the learned professions have their national organizations, the annual meetings of which give the opportunity for exchanging specialized information, learning of experimental work done by colleagues at other institutions, and discussing the present state and future development of the field. Governmental and industrial needs have understandably increased the opportunity of scientist and social scientist to undertake special missions, attend conferences national or international in scope, and work with colleagues from all parts of the world on special enterprises ranging from the development of underprivileged areas to problems of medical care at high altitudes, field work in oil geology, setting up a banking system in a new nation, or working with a UNESCO committee on the refugee problem.[6] No one in any way, shape, or manner begrudges these experts their fine opportunities, honorable alike to them and to the United States. Humanists occasionally have similar chances, but in a world wherein cultural tensions and cultural misunderstandings seem to increase, humanists have not characteristically enjoyed a wide range of such opportunities. Only recently has the American Council of Learned Societies received modest temporary funds with which to

[6] The IGY (International Geophysical Year) is a remarkable example of this sort of internationalization of scientific effort.

send American representatives to international conferences and to assist in bringing occasional international
conferences to the United States.[7]

Money is needed to finance a far greater number of
local and regional conferences among humanists than is
now possible. Existing regional bodies like the Southern
Humanities Conference are so scandalously underfinanced
that they have had on occasion to shut up shop. Money is
needed to enable the great special libraries of the country,
such as the Henry E. Huntington Library at San Marino,
the William L. Clements Library at Ann Arbor, the library of the American Antiquarian Society at Worcester,
the John Pierpont Morgan Library in New York, and so
on,[8] to stage conferences of scholars competent to discuss
the best ways of exploiting the materials, and, in the next
place, in many cases, to provide stipends ample enough to
bring superior specialists to the collections in the same
way that, for example, scientists are brought to the Weiz-
mann Institute. What is true of libraries is equally true
of museums. Money is needed for summer institutes in
the humanities. There are at present few such institutes—
the annual English Institute at Columbia and the Linguistic Institute being examples of one sort, writers' conferences being examples of a second, and various summer
schools or summer seminars in foreign languages, archaeology, and so forth being examples of a third type. But
these are not numerous. Moreover, writers' conferences,

---

[7] In this latter activity the Social Science Research Council joins in
directing the expenditure of funds.

[8] Besides these independent libraries one thinks also of great collections
found in general academic libraries, such as the Wrenn Library and the
Garcia collection at the University of Texas, the collection of Southern
historical materials at the University of North Carolina library, the working papers of recent and contemporary poets at Buffalo, and so forth.
But to list the treasures available in American libraries is an impossible
task; the real problem is to free scholars from other chores in order that
they may use the materials available.

whatever they do for literature, do little or nothing for scholarship, and summer schools and summer seminars commonly charge fees and require the scholar who enrolls in them to pay for his keep during the session. The present program for the improvement of science teaching in the secondary schools (and beyond), in contrast, sends the teacher-scientist to a summer institute at small expense to himself, a privilege the teacher-scholar does not enjoy. One of the benefits money could confer upon humanistic scholars would be the creation of a score of summer study institutes properly endowed, each in the vicinity of a great library, museum, or other center of source materials here or abroad. At such a summer study institute in the humanities forty or fifty scholars chosen on a merit basis, their expenses paid, and free of all other duties for the summer, could pursue researches that would add to their own professional status, enrich their capacity as teachers, and vastly increase in depth and range that priceless national possession, humane learning.

5. *Permanent Institutes.* The country has seen with pride the creation of the Princeton Institute for Advanced Study, with which the name of Einstein will be forever associated. This is on the Atlantic seaboard. On the Pacific Coast is the Center for Advanced Study in the Behavioral Sciences. Distinguished names in the humanities have been associated with both these establishments, but neither of them is mainly or exclusively devoted to advancing the cause of the humanities, and the Pacific Coast institution is by definition principally concerned with the social sciences and psychology. The country needs parallel institutions for the humanistic disciplines, one in the Far West, one in the Middle West, one in the South, and one in the East, each located near first-class libraries and museums, each sufficiently well endowed to maintain a competent director and a small, well-chosen staff, and each rich

enough in income to offer twenty or thirty fellowships annually to first-class scholars desirous of completing a major piece of investigation. Such institutions would cost money, but they cannot be dismissed as utopian fantasies in a country which has created and paid for the Palomar telescope, the Dumbarton Oaks project in Byzantine history, the Brookhaven laboratories, the Metropolitan Museum of Art, the Widener Library, the Boston Symphony Orchestra, the Bay Bridge at San Francisco, the national park system, the Metropolitan Opera, the National Gallery in Washington, and much else.

We must think of the humanities, humane learning, and humanistic scholarship in terms consonant with a nation of almost 175 million people. It is not in any way excessive to say that, in order to attain this end, we ought immediately to increase our support of these great activities by at least fifty million dollars a year—and then go on from there.